CREATIVE IN THE IMAGE OF GOD

CREATIVE IN THE IMAGE OF GOD

An Aesthetic Practical Theology of Young Adult Faith

Katherine M. Douglass

 CASCADE *Books* · Eugene, Oregon

CREATIVE IN THE IMAGE OF GOD
An Aesthetic Practical Theology of Young Adult Faith

Cascade Books
An Imprint of Wipf and Stock Publishers
199 W. 8th Ave., Suite 3
Eugene, OR 97401

www.wipfandstock.com

PAPERBACK ISBN: 978-1-5326-8453-1
HARDCOVER ISBN: 978-1-5326-8454-8
EBOOK ISBN: 978-1-5326-8455-5

Cataloguing-in-Publication data:

Names: Douglass, Katherine M., 1981–, author.

Title: Creative in the image of God : an aesthetic practical theology of young adult faith / Katherine M. Douglass.

Description: Eugene, OR : Cascade Books, 2020 | Includes bibliographical references.

Identifiers: ISBN 978-1-5326-8453-1 (paperback) | ISBN 978-1-5326-8454-8 (hardcover) | ISBN 978-1-5326-8455-5 (ebook)

Subjects: LCSH: Spiritual formation. | Young adults—Religious life. | Church work with young adults. | Christianity and the arts.

Classification: BV4511 .D68 2020 (paperback) | BV4511 .D68 (ebook)

Manufactured in the U.S.A.   02/27/20

This book is dedicated to my husband, John,
and to our sons, George, Paul, and Will Douglass,
and to my parents, Dorothy and Bill Lewis.

In every generation, may love increase.

Well, science is the theology of our time, and like the old theology it's a muddle of conflicting assertions. What gripes my gut is that it has such a miserable vocabulary and such a pallid pack of images to offer to us—to the humble laity—for our edification and our faith. The old priest in his black robe gave us things that seemed to have concrete existence; you prayed to the Mother of God and somebody had given you an image that looked just right for the Mother of God. The new priest in his whitish lab-coat gives you nothing at all except a constantly changing vocabulary which he—because he usually doesn't know any Greek—can't pronounce, and you are expected to trust him implicitly because he knows what you are too dumb to comprehend. It's the most overweening, pompous priesthood mankind has ever endured in all its recorded history, and its lack of symbol and metaphor and its zeal for abstraction drive mankind to a barren land of starved imagination.

—Arthur, to his wife, Maria,
a mystically oriented New Testament Professor,
in Robertson Davies' *What's Bred in the Bone*

CONTENTS

ACKNOWLEDGMENTS

This work has been a labor of love. First, I must thank my devoted partner, John, who personally knows the joys and challenges of academic research. We have been on this journey together and I could not have done it alone. My three sons, George, Paul, and Will, were all born during this project and they give me healthy perspective on what really matters in life. They have also increased my capacity to love. My parents, Dorothy and Bill Lewis, contributed their expertise and support to this project in ways that are immeasurable and yet pervasive throughout this book. Thank you for a lifetime of support.

It is with great admiration that I thank Gordon Mikoski, my dissertation advisor and mentor, who encouraged me to pursue practical theological topics that were deep within my heart and to whom I owe at least a thousand red pens. Thanks also go to Kenda Creasy Dean, my mentor who embodied the beautiful integrity of being a mother, pastor, and academic. I must thank Richard Osmer, who ensured that I had the skills and tools to conduct rigorous qualitative research while retaining a sensitivity to the work of the Holy Spirit. Finally, Robert Wuthnow not only shared his wisdom with me but also welcomed me into the sociology of religion community at Princeton University, all of whom provided helpful critique and perspective.

I had the joy and fortune of being in a dissertation writing group with women whom I continue to admire deeply as they teach around the globe: Elaine James, Sonia Waters, Lisa Bowens, Mary Schmidt, Janette Ok, Oan Jaisaodee, and Jin Park. This book would not have come into being without your encouragement and loving presence in my life. I also had the privilege of being counted among the Timothy Scholars, a hilarious crew of earnest practical theologians who lead through their service: Drew Dyson, Jason Santos, Amanda Drury, Andrew Zirschkey, Stephen Cady, Christiane Lang Hearlson, Blair Bertrand, and Nate Stucky.

I must also thank my brilliant theologically minded friends who have discussed art, theology, and young adults with me as we ran half-marathons, walked the Camino, hiked, camped, and feasted over Thanksgiving dinner. Shannon Smythe, Deb Ondrasik, Trina Terrion, Lisa Vick, Janine Edwards, Tara Woodard-Lehman, Tanya Cordoba, and Jennifer Jenkins Gill, I am so lucky to call you my friends. Finally, I want to thank artist and theologian Shannon Sigler for being my first friend in Seattle and also making beautiful art, including *Lap Full of Words*, the charcoal drawing that is on the cover of this book.

Learning from the thirty young adults in this study shaped not only this book but also the way that I teach. I continue to learn from the young adults at Seattle Pacific University and hope to faithfully listen to them as they seek out God. In this book and in all things, to God be the glory.

INTRODUCTION

Reinforcing the epigram that opens this book, a 2019 Gallup poll found that respect for clergy and institutional religion is at an all-time low, yet human longing for divine encounter persists.[1] What is it about the aesthetic dimension of religious practice, in the form of concrete existence, symbol, metaphor, and imagination, that edifies faith to make it seem "just right"? In his book *What's Bred in the Bone*, Robertson Davies ponders this question through the interactions of the aesthetic, academic, and spiritual lives of his characters. Similar to Davies, I have sought to discover how the arts edify the faith lives of young adults. Through interviews with thirty young adults about their faith, I learned that the arts facilitate transformative experiences of connection, expression, and opening. Like Davies, I am critical of the overly linguistic epistemology of the Reformed tradition and instead propose a practical theology that emphasizes embodied and aesthetic dimensions of knowing as practical reason.

Young adulthood has fascinated theologians, researchers, marketers, and the artistic world for centuries. The "coming-of-age" novel, where a character enters the wild world of familial independence, ideological freedom, and sexual awakening, has captured our collective imagination and has been glamorized as the "Odyssey Years."[2] These are the years of life where anything is possible and there are seemingly no consequences. Sociologists and demographers such as Katherine Newman, Robert Wuthnow, Jean Twenge, Jeffrey Jensen Arnett, Christian Smith, and Frank Furstenberg have shown, however, that for many, these years include existential questioning,

---

1. Newport, "Why Are Americans Losing Respect for Organized Religion?"
2. Brooks, "The Odyssey Years."

relational longing, and a significant decrease in religious participation. These trends correlate with, and are perhaps exacerbated by, the introduction and widespread use of smartphones and social media as well as a general malaise toward organized religion.[3] Despite those who claim that there is real participation and real community among these online communities, there are also alarming trends that correlate with increased online use.[4] Correlating effects include an in increase in mental illness and a decrease in congregational participation.[5] The inverse has been shown to be true as well: "devoted" and "regular" congregational participation correlates with feeling happy, understood, and seen.[6] Rather than going out to encounter and experience the world, many young adults stay home in the evenings, scrolling through their feed, watching the "few" go out to do, make, explore, and create . . . and then post on Instagram, Twitter, or Snapchat. New media seems to have created a spectator class of this generation—a league of "viewers" who "like" and curate an online presence with more online engagement and fewer embodied encounters.

There does, however, seem to be resistance to an overly virtual existence—spending six or more hours "online" daily.[7] Those who engage in the "play" and re-creation of artmaking or aesthetic encounter embody this resistance. There are, of course, other embodied activities that affirm the embodied reality of young adults; however, for this study, the focus was on the role of the arts and their relationship to faith. Among those young adults whom I interviewed, specifically asking about the role that the arts play in their faith lives, I found that their aesthetic participation seemed to directly resist the disembodied, virtual, antisocial behaviors that define the dominant trends among this population. Out of those interviewed, all but one claimed that their participation in the arts allowed them to express their identity and feel known, to connect with others both in the present and across time, and also to open up to new ideas about God. All of this, in spite of generational trends that would suggest otherwise. So what are we to make of this exceptionalism?

3. Twenge, *iGen*, 49–68.

4. Jenkins, *Confronting the Challenges of Participatory Culture*; Zirsky, *Beyond the Screen*.

5. Twenge, *iGen*, 93–95.

6. Smith, *Souls in Transition*, 267.

7. Twenge, *iGen*, 51.

In this book, I claim that the arts provide an embodied way of knowing—an aesthetic practical reason. Aesthetic practical reason affirms the bodily ways of knowing that God created humanity to have. Embodied ways of knowing are not simple but complicated, often holding multiple realities that seem to be in tension. This is seen clearly in the arts, which are both deeply personal and open for interpretation by an "other." The arts are specific to a time and place while being able to speak across time and space. They also embody and give voice to the philosophical, epistemological, and political power of an individual despite their age, class, race, or gender. The arts—not merely high art but art created by anyone—provide an embodied way of knowing.

This research was collected through interviews and takes a grounded theory approach to learn from young adults. Grounded theory begins with an open-ended question. In this study I asked, "What role do the arts play in your faith life?" The theoretical answer to the question emerges from the patterns and trends among the responses of the participants in the study.

What I learned from listening to these thirty Presbyterian young adults is that the arts connect young adults to others and to God; participation in the arts helps young adults express their identity; and finally, encounters with art open young adults to God and God's presence in their lives.

Building on this grounded theory, I will show the relationship of this theory to aesthetic learning theory. I review and critique a Reformed aesthetic theology to provide a resource for those interested in shifting the "way of knowing" in Christian life away from its historically linguistic center toward an embodied form of practical reason—an aesthetic practical theology.

One unique feature of this book is that it shares the voices of the young adults who have been or are currently connected with congregations. Unlike other national studies (such as the National Study of Youth and Religion, led by Christian Smith), which expose a decline in congregational activity and theological articulacy among young people, this book highlights exceptional individuals who have articulate theological beliefs and opinions and who regularly or semi-regularly attend worship. According to Smith's categories, these are the "devoted" and "regulars."[8] In order to remain vital (and dare I suggest faithful?), congregations ought to consider the experience of those young adults who have chosen to remain connected to local religious communities, rather than lamenting the absence of those not present. Additionally, ministers and congregational

8. Smith, *Souls in Transition*, 211–23.

leaders need to consider how to minister alongside young adults amid the real and unique challenges they face.

AN OUTLINE OF THIS BOOK

In the first chapter, "Changing Landscapes of Young Adulthood," I provide a review of current research on young adults from the fields of psychology and sociology that shows how I came to my research question. In this chapter, I show four key features of young adulthood. These are patterns that have been seen in every generation but seem to be more pronounced with each younger generation. First, young adults are spending more time in young adulthood than previous generations. Second, this is significant because young adulthood is the least religious period of a person's life. Third, despite a lack of traditionally measured religious participation, young adults are very interested in matters of faith, spirituality, and religion. Fourth, young adults are more aesthetically attuned and oriented than previous generations. These four features of young adulthood provide the rationale for this research study.

In the second chapter, "Art Connects, Expresses, and Opens," I report the findings of a grounded theory study that I conducted in 2011. I conducted thirty interviews to gain understanding into the role that the arts play in the faith lives of young adults. My main finding was that the arts play a "significant" role in the faith lives of young adults, as they foster connection, expression, and opening.

In the third chapter, "Recovering the Aesthetic Dimension of Practical Reason," I analyze these findings through the lens of aesthetic learning theory to conclude that the arts are a form of practical reason, or embodied and integrated philosophical thinking. Through their participation in the arts as practical reason, young adults are transformed as they critique, record, interpret, and reimagine the world, God, and themselves.

In chapter 4, "The Image of God, Art, and Christian Formation," I consider these claims in light of the Reformed tradition, which has historically had deep reticence regarding the arts and the Christian life. In this section, I identify the powerful potential of the arts to form (or, as John Calvin and Karl Barth claimed, malform) the faith of young adults. Following this, I use the work of John Dillenberger to argue that the epistemological possibilities for Christian formation are expanded when the arts are employed. Finally, I use the work of Wentzel van Huyssteen to claim that the activity of making art is an expression of the *imago Dei* and has inherent value.

In the fifth chapter, "An Aesthetic Practical Theology of Young Adult Faith," I interpret the meaning of this grounded theory for ministers, teachers, and practical theologians by appropriating insights from culturally responsive teaching theory.

SOME BRIEF DEFINITIONS OF IMPORTANT TERMINOLOGY

"Young Adults"

There have been significant and meaningful debates around what to call this stage of life, this generation, or this cohort of people who are between the ages of eighteen and thirty-something. Jeffrey Arnett, using Erik Erikson's framework from the field of psychology, considers many of these labels in the introduction of his book *Emerging Adulthood*, and, as his title suggests, he proposes new terminology: "emerging adulthood."[9] Rather than following Arnett, as Chris Smith does in *Souls in Transition*, I have chosen to retain the language of "young adult."[10] I have made this choice for a few reasons.

First, Arnett claims that he has chosen the term "emerging" because it is "a better descriptive term for the exploratory, unstable, fluid quality of the period."[11] I believe that this claim is accurate if we are discussing only upper- and middle-class American young adults, as well as some Western countries throughout the world. Other studies, such as those by sociologist Katherine Newman, present a much more complicated landscape of those in their young adult years.[12] Unlike many young adults who are experiencing high mobility, transition, and feeling "in-between," Newman identifies various countries where young adults feel stuck, infantilized, or even identify as adults while they are still chronologically in their teenage years. I believe these young adults are present within the United States as well.

Additionally, Arnett admits that his definition is of a very specific group, and once someone is married, has a child, or depends completely

9. Arnett, *Emerging Adulthood*, 17–21.

10. Smith, *Souls in Transition*, 6.

11. Arnett, *Emerging Adulthood*, 18.

12. Newman, "Ties That Bind," 645–69; Newman, *The Accordion Family*.

upon their own income they are no longer an emerging adult. In my quantitative and qualitative research I have included the voices of those who have children, who are married, and who make 100 percent of their own income. For these reasons, I have chosen to use the term "young adult" to refer to this group.

"The Arts"

Throughout this research study I talk a lot about "the arts." Rather than going into this research with a predetermined definition of art, I have allowed the language world of young adults to shape and form this definition. As a result, the definition of "the arts" will become most apparent in the third chapter, which shares many quotes from young adults in which they use this term. I have made this choice in an attempt to be faithful to the grounded theory approach that I have taken. This approach invites various findings and definitions to emerge from the research process.[13] As a result, the working definition of "the arts" used by young adults included dance, singing, painting, poetry, and music—as we might expect—but it also included "step" dancing, working as a disc jockey, blogging, playing online games, being in nature, and reading novels.

"Faith," "Spirituality," and "Religion"

In my research I never once heard the claim "I am spiritual but not religious." I did find, as is reported in chapter 3, some disillusionment with churches alongside high levels of interest in faith, devotional practices, and spirituality. The phrase "I am spiritual but not religious" seems to connote having an interest in mystical and spiritual experience, while wanting to distance oneself from Jesus Christ, the Holy Spirit, and God the Father and Creator. My findings completely disagree with this, likely, in part, due to the study participants' upbringing or current participation in Presbyterian Church (USA) congregations. Young adults in this study used the Christian language of being created in the image of God. They claimed that they saw the Holy Spirit at work in their lives when they were doing creative things. One young woman suggested that I title this research project "Creative Christ." I believe that the correct interpretation of this is that young adults

13. Creswell, *Qualitative Inquiry and Research Design*, 86.

are highly interested in embodying their Christian faith, not merely knowing about being a Christian.

Looking at the semantic use of the terms "spiritual," "faith," and "religious" was not the goal of this project, and so I only comment on it here briefly in order to preemptively answer the question that some may have as they read through this research. Similar to my approach with using the term "art," I attempted to use whatever language for faith, spirituality, devotion, or religion that the young adult whom I was interviewing used. Most used all of the terms with varying degrees of fluidity.

"Formation" and "Transformation"

There has been a historical debate regarding how God works in the faith lives of individuals. Some, such as John Westerhoff and Horace Bushnell, have argued that God "forms" individuals through families and communities.[14] Others, such as James Loder and Andrew Root, follow Søren Kierkegaard in arguing that through disruptive experiences, often marked by a crisis, individuals are transformed by the Holy Spirit.[15] I believe that the Holy Spirit both forms and transforms people. I believe that this happens through habits, rituals, and cultural acquisition as well as surprising and unexpected experiences. I have used both terms throughout this book. I have used the term "formation" when focusing on the human dimension of teaching and forming individuals (which, I believe, is guided and led by the Holy Spirit). I have used the term "transformation" when referring to change that can only come about as a result of the work of the Holy Spirit and that was in no way prepared for or predicted by human planning—where there is deep, fundamental change regarding an individual's self-understanding or relationship to others, the world, or God. The only section where this is not the case is when I engage the work of Maxine Greene. Greene is a self-proclaimed atheist and believes that religion oppresses individuals. She uses the term "transformation" to refer to something akin to self-actualization.

14. Bushnell, *Christian Nurture*; Westerhoff, *Will Our Children Have Faith?*
15. Loder, *The Logic of the Spirit*; Root, *Revisiting Relational Youth Ministry.*

Methodology

The qualitative data gathered through this project in the form of interviews has been interpreted within the framework of grounded theory. The grounded theory approach has been used within a practical theological framework and is informed by the Reformed tradition. This is evident in the way that I have engaged the fields of psychology and sociology as dialogue partners as data was initially gathered and interpreted. I have critically appropriated aesthetic learning theory in order to analyze and understand the role that the arts play in the faith lives of young adults. I normatively and critically engage the Reformed theological tradition to critique and to gain insight into the claims of this research. Finally, I propose the grounded theory that participation in the arts functions as a theologically rich experience of practical reason wherein the Christian identity of young adults is transformed as they connect, express, and open through their participation in art.

1

CHANGING LANDSCAPES
OF YOUNG ADULTHOOD

This chapter presents the current research on young adulthood from the fields of psychology and sociology. This is done to in order to problematize current claims regarding the lack of religiosity among young adults. I will offer evidence to the contrary and argue for a more nuanced interpretation of general trends—that young adulthood is a time of spiritual discernment that is sometimes worked out through participation in the arts. This claim connects with the overarching thesis of this book by showing that the young adult years are a time of high spiritual interest and discernment regarding one's religious identity. This claim also sets the stage for the following chapter, which elaborates on the role that the arts play in the faith lives of young adults: to foster connection, expression, and opening.

My empirical research study focused on the question, What role do the arts play in the faith lives of young adults? This chapter reviews contemporary research on young adults, highlighting the changing landscape of young adulthood. This review will provide foundational knowledge about young adults and expose some tensions in current research. This chapter will also expose the experiences of the current cohort that make them especially creative.

Since the publication in 2004 of Jeffrey Arnett's *Emerging Adulthood: The Winding Road from the Late Teens through the Twenties* there has been increased attention from researchers, churches, and the media given to the life stage of young adulthood.[1] This age range has long been acknowledged as a time of transition and major life decisions. This is traditionally the period when individuals move away from home, consider and decide on a career and spouse, and become financially independent from their parents. Whether we call it "emerging adulthood" (Arnett), "later adulthood" (Erik Erikson), or simply "young adulthood," there is general consensus among psychologists and sociologists that this period of life is changing in significant ways.

A LIVELY CONVERSATION ON YOUNG ADULTHOOD

In my review of psychological and sociological research on young adults I identified four themes of young adulthood. While some of these themes have been seen in previous generations, they seem to be more pronounced with younger generational cohorts. This is happening not only in the United States (although that will be the focus of this research) but internationally as well.[2]

The first theme within the scope of the changing landscape of young adulthood is taking form in time. The years one spends in young adulthood are expanding, extending into the late twenties and early thirties. Sociologists and psychologists speculate on the reasons for these changes: longer life span, greater support from parents, or lazy young adults. Common to all is the claim that this stage of life is lengthening. A second theme is that young adulthood is the least religious period of a person's life. This is borne out in both national and denominational research through studies that focus on religious participation, including Bible reading, frequency of prayer, and congregational involvement. The third theme, especially interesting considering the second, is that this lack of church attendance and involvement does not completely correlate with a decrease in interest in matters of faith, religion, and spirituality. The fourth theme is that this generation of young adults is more aesthetically attuned and oriented than past generations, and this is often expressed in their faith lives. This final theme was identified in a preliminary way in the work of sociologist Robert Wuthnow

1. Arnett, *Emerging Adulthood.*

2. Katherine Newman provides a sociological look at the recent trends among young adults internationally, specifically with regard to changing economic, social, and political pressures. Newman, *The Accordion Family.*

and has been further explored and confirmed in my own research. Inquiry into this fourth theme is the focus of this study.[3]

Igniting the Conversation: Life Cycle Theory

Before giving greater attention to these four thematic trends with young adults I will offer a critique of Arnett's life cycle theory.[4] I start with Arnett because, as mentioned above, he has been one of the most prominent voices drawing attention to the changing landscape of young adulthood. Some developmental theories, such as life cycle theory, tend toward the straightforward clarity of categorizing life. Life stages, as Erik Erikson lays them out, are a prime example of this. While Erikson's stages allow for overlap, flexibility, and a return to past stages if the need arises, the general focus is on steps, or stages, through which each human goes with little attention to global, economic, political, or social forces, trends, and events. Life stage theory focuses on the individual human, rather than the individual within society. This makes sense because Arnett and Erikson are in the field of psychology, which is more concerned with the psychic development of individuals, in contrast to sociology, which is more concerned with people groups. It is for this reason that I believe Arnett's contribution is limited and fails to account for the significant impact that the changing landscape of social institutions can have on a generation.

Take, for example, those who came of age during a military draft. Not only are the lives of drafted young men affected but also the young women, who may find their participation in marriage or childbirth delayed or rushed

---

3. Wuthnow, *All in Sync*; Wuthnow, *After the Baby Boomers.*

4. Authors use three terms when considering the psychosocial development of an individual, and due to their similarity those terms are worth defining here for the sake of clarity. (1) Life *cycle* theory is most strongly associated with Erik Erikson, a psychologist whose work focused on the psychological and relational changes through which an individual goes over the course of their life. Arnett writes within this tradition. See Erikson, *Identity and the Life Cycle.* (2) Life *stage* is a term employed by Erikson and Arnett to distinguish different periods throughout the life cycle. Erikson's research divides the normal human life into eight stages through which each individual progresses as they age. Arnett's thesis is that the current experience of young adults places "identity exploration" in the sixth rather than fifth stage. The sixth stage, emerging adulthood, is a new stage proposed by Arnett based on his research. (3) Life *course* theory is associated with Glen Elder, who researched the effect of the Great Depression on children. This theory gives greater attention to the social, historical, economic, and familial forces in the life of an individual than life cycle theory. Elder, *Children of the Great Depression.*

due to the two-year service commitment of a generation of young men. Taking a governmental policy, such as a draft, into account offers insight into social phenomena such as the "baby boom," which impacted both individuals and communities. Using only the lens of life cycle theory limits the scope of our view. For this reason, I believe life course theory gives greater nuance and depth of insight into unique challenges or characteristics of young adulthood, especially when attempting to draw attention to the changes taking place specifically for those born after 1981.[5] Ultimately, I believe Arnett's insights come from considering the effects of social, economic, and global trends despite his use of life cycle terminology.

Nuancing the Conversation: Life Course Theory

Glen Elder initiated life course theory in his 1974 work *Children of the Great Depression*, which became a model and resource for social workers when trying to intervene in the lives of individuals.[6] According to Elder, when used as a developmental theory, life course theory includes "the recognition that individual lives are influenced by their ever-changing historical context, that the study of human lives calls for new ways of thinking about their pattern and dynamic, and that concepts of human development should apply to processes across the life span."[7] According to sociologist Elizabeth Hutchison, this method of assessing individuals was initially developed for the field of social work, for people who were looking to advise or intervene in the lives of individuals who are faced with challenges.[8] The categories used by life course theory are helpful because they draw attention to events happening in culture, social pressures, and the interdependence of lives and family relationships that all have important influence and impact on the life of an individual. Arnett gives some attention to these; however, life course theory emphasizes the cohort effect of specific trends with greater perspicuity than life cycle theory allows. For example, rather than simply relying on age, life course theory divides the timing of life into categories:

- *chronological age* is measured by one's birthdate;

5. See footnote 4 for a brief definition of "life cycle theory," "life stages," and "life course theory."

6. Elder, *Children of the Great Depression*.

7. Elder, "Life Course as Developmental Theory," 1–12.

8. Hutchison, *Dimensions of Human Behavior*.

- *biological age* is measured by the age of one's body—for example, if a person is a smoker, then their body may be "older" than their chronological age;

- *psychological age* is measured by the age one feels oneself to be—as Arnett found, many young adults in their late twenties feel "younger," while those in their late teens and early twenties feel "older";[9]

- *social age* is measured by societal expectations for an individual—these are sometimes formal, such as the legal age for driving, voting, consuming alcohol, or military service, and sometimes informal, such as the age by which one is expected to finish school, "settle down," or get married;[10]

- *spiritual age* measures maturity in the spiritual life.[11]

These categories allow for a thicker and more nuanced level of description, without which comments on "age" become somewhat haphazard or arbitrary. In my research, viewing young adults through the categories of chronological age, psychological age, and social age will provide greater understanding of the spiritual lives of young adults. The category of spiritual age is somewhat challenging to determine. In some ways, spiritual maturity seems to depend on the resources and communities available to an individual, and yet there are distinct exceptions in this system, as some individuals are raised in congregations where they are surrounded by opportunities for spiritual growth but the outcome of their faith is highly unpredictable. There are also people who have only been tangentially related to religious institutions but who have profoundly deep spiritual lives.[12] While this has been a lively debate, a definition of spiritual age and maturity will not be attempted here. Instead, I will look at levels of interest in spirituality, faith, and religion.

9. Ninety percent of young adults report feeling like an adult by the age of thirty. Those in their twenties, however, do not predictably feel more adult as they age. According to Arnett, "There are 21-year-olds who say they have definitely reached adulthood, and 28-year-olds who say they still feel in between" (*Emerging Adulthood*, 218).

10. Most young adults interviewed by Arnett identified the age of thirty as the point at which they planned to get married. Arnett, *Emerging Adulthood*, 102–4.

11. Hutchison, *Dimensions of Human Behavior*, 22–23; Fowler, *Stages of Faith*. Hutchison recognizes this category but says little other than to mention James Fowler and Erik Erikson as two who acknowledge and, in the case of Fowler, develop this schema.

12. James Loder's work *Logic of the Spirit* breaks from stage theory and emphasizes the "illogical" logic of the work of the Holy Spirit in the life of an individual.

In her article "Ties That Bind: Cultural Interpretations of Delayed Adulthood in Western Europe and Japan," Katherine S. Newman uses life course theory to analyze similar and dissonant trends among young adults in a variety of cultures around the world.[13] One difference among cultures that Newman highlights relates to attitudes toward the young adults who are living at home. The questions "Who is to blame (or praise) for this?" and "How do we feel about this trend?" underlie Arnett's research, which are explicitly exposed in Newman's research. Ultimately, I believe Arnett's 2004 publication places blame for the trends of young adulthood on fun-loving, "self-focused" young adults. He does acknowledge some societal trends; however, the attitude at the end seems to be, "Who would complain about more free time? Clearly, they like it this way. Wouldn't we all want to extend our young adult years, and live with fewer rather than more responsibilities, if we had the chance?"[14] It seems overly optimistic to assume that young adults are quite happy as they meander through unstable

13. Rather than merely looking at statistics showing the number of young adults who live at home with their parents, Newman explores the interconnectedness between generations as they seek to explain why this trend is occurring. Despite the similar lengthening of time young adults spend living at home, explanations as to the source of this phenomenon vary greatly. For example, she finds that Spanish mothers are happy to have their beloved children live at home, and they blame governmental policies for their children's inability to find a job. Japanese mothers, however, are embarrassed by their "freeters" (the Japanese name for young adults who are not pursuing higher education or work and are living at home) and blame a surplus of choice, absentee fathers, and overly doting mothers for their children's "failure to launch."

To gain greater insight into these trends, Newman explores the economic and governmental history of both Spain and Japan. In Japan, an economic crisis during the 1990s had the effect of shrinking the job market, resulting in fewer jobs for those entering the market at that time. In Spain, with the end of Francisco Franco's authoritarian rule in 1975 came an end to laws influenced by Roman Catholic morals, meaning that birth control was suddenly legal, as was cohabitation. This was quickly followed by new governmental policies that allowed for contract and part-time laborers (as opposed to the previous practice of hiring individuals only under full-time status). Knowledge of these governmental and economic shifts shed light on the plurality of causes behind the lengthening of time a young adult may live at home. This research also highlights the significance of the narrative that is told to explain these trends. Newman believes that neither governmental blame in Spain nor self-blame in Japan gives a full account of the main causes for changing trends. Newman, "Ties That Bind," 645–69.

14. According to Arnett young adults long to stay in this stage because "the responsibilities of adulthood can be onerous and stressful, and emerging adults sometimes look back with nostalgia on a childhood and adolescence that seems easier in some ways than their lives now." Arnett, *Emerging Adulthood*, 228; Dankosky, "Emerging Adults."

employment or underemployment—or worse, unemployment—as well as low-commitment relationships and living with their parents. Societally, it seems that we have shifted from being jealous of the freedom and youthful beauty of young adults to feeling sorry for them after the 2010 census results were published. In his recent media appearances, Arnett has clearly acknowledged these shifts and seems to have tempered his interpretation.[15] There are outliers, however, as one man in a seminar I led on young adults said, "My daughter is in this age range and when she comes to visit for the weekend she clears out our cupboards and takes whatever she wants from our pantry. This generation thinks they are entitled to whatever they want!"[16] Rather than interpreting his daughter's actions as securing her need for food, possibly in light of financial strain, he assumed that she was essentially stealing from her own father. This father's question illustrates the generational difference of expectations regarding social age.

In what follows, I will agree with much of what Arnett has written regarding trends and shifts in what he calls emerging adulthood. I will often, however, use the categories of life course theory to gain greater insight into changing trends. Sociological studies will aid these efforts by providing insight into this age demographic and the unique societal changes affecting young adults. When economic trends such as the Great Recession and social trends such as the delayed retirement of many baby boomers are taken into account, certain trends in young adults, such as the delay of selecting a lifelong career, are understood in a far more nuanced light.[17] That young adults are not "motivated" or that they prefer a carefree lifestyle is no longer a satisfying explanation for changes in young adulthood when viewed through the lens of life course theory.

Rather than starting with historical, political, and sociological phenomena, as Smith and Wuthnow do, I will embed comments on life course events within the research I report in a style similar to Newman, who allows questions about social trends to arise from her findings.[18] The

15. Jeffrey Arnett's webpage, accessed January 7, 2012.

16. Douglass, "Psychological and Sociological Landscapes of Young Adulthood," presentation for Saturdays@Princeton, November 5, 2011.

17. Pew Research Center, "Recession Turns a Graying Office Grayer."

18. Sociologist Christian Smith prefaces his research in *Souls in Transition* by giving an overview of the historical context of young adults with reference to life course theory. Similarly, Wuthnow includes a chapter on "The Changing Life Worlds of Young Adults" before reporting his own research. Smith and Snell, *Souls in Transition*; Wuthnow, *After the Baby Boomers*, 20–49.

pattern of my reporting will first give an overview of sociological studies already done on young adults, followed by the results of my research.

THEME ONE: YOUNG ADULTHOOD IS LENGTHENING

Whereas Erikson stated that early adulthood lasts from eighteen to twenty-two, Arnett's study included those ages twenty to twenty-nine, the age period he defines as emerging adulthood.[19] For psychologists, chronological age is not necessarily the most important factor in determining life stage. Arnett adds the caveat (and Erikson would agree) that an individual may be within this stage of life far beyond the age of twenty-nine: into one's thirties, forties, or even fifties.[20] The categories of life course theory help clarify that this lengthening has as much to do with psychological and social age as chronological age. There continues to be much speculation as to the many potential causes behind the lengthening of young adulthood as well as the impact of this lengthening on various dimensions of our social life together as a society.

According to Arnett, there is a limit to this period of life. The traditional boundaries of this period, however, have been extended to a time later in life. While it was common for young men in the 1950s to marry around the age of twenty-two and young women around the age of twenty, these ages have increased by about one year over each span of twenty years.[21] According to the 2010 census, the average age of marriage for women was twenty-six, and for men it was twenty-eight.[22] The average time for having a first child remains constant in relation to the year one marries, at about one year after marriage.

Arnett points to birth control, increased levels of higher education, and changes in women's roles at home and in the workplace as causes for this increase. These trends are also confirmed by sociologist Frank Furstenberg.[23] Referencing the work of Gavin W. Jones and Wei-Jun Jean Yeung, Furstenberg shows that the rising age of first marriage is not unique to the

19. Arnett, *Emerging Adulthood*, 24.

20. Arnett, *Emerging Adulthood*, vi.

21. U.S. Census Bureau, "Estimated Median Age at First Marriage, by Sex: 1890 to Present."

22. U.S. Census Bureau, "Estimated Median Age of First Marriage, by Sex: 1890 to Present."

23. Furstenberg, "Family Change in Global Perspective."

United States but is a global trend, with a few significant exceptions, such as most of India, China, Indonesia, and Vietnam.[24] The average life expectancy for men and women has also increased. In 1950, the average life expectancy in the United States for men was 65.6, and for women it was 71.1.[25] By 2010, the average life expectancy for men was 75.7, and for women 80.8.[26] And the most recent charts from 2016 show the average life expectancy for males at 76.2 and for females at 81.1.[27] Average life expectancy over the last sixty years has increased around ten years for both men and women. Whereas a person born in the 1950s would be "middle-aged" by the age of thirty-three or thirty-four, young adults today are "middle-aged" when they are thirty-eight or thirty-nine, although it is unlikely that living longer affects the way young adults feel about their age. Furstenberg and others have found a general global decline in fertility, with the exception of rural Africa and parts of the Middle East.[28] One contributor to this trend may be the availability of in vitro fertilization and other medical therapies available to aid older women in having children. Knowing that these therapies are available may reinforce a woman's choice to delay having children.

In 2009, sociologist Simone Scherger conducted a cohort study within the life course tradition. Her study examined the effects of governmental and societal institutions on trends among young adults in West Germany.[29] She looked at trends surrounding the average age of departure from home, marriage, and having a first child. Among her most significant findings was that economic, societal, familial, and individual factors influence these points of transition in the life of a young adult. Scherger differentiates between the influence of primary institutions, such as governmental policies on the legal driving age, and secondary institutions, such as business employment and economic conditions, which may dictate the reality of the job market. She explains,

24. Furstenberg, "Family Change in Global Perspective," 8; Jones and Yeung, "Marriage in Asia."

25. "Life Expectancy: United States," available at http://www.data360.org/dsg.aspx?Data_Set_Group_Id=195.

26. U.S. Census Bureau, "Expectation of Life at Birth, 1960 to 2008, and Projections, 2010 to 2020."

27. Arias, Xu, and Kochanek, "United States Life Tables, 2016."

28. Furstenberg, "Family Change in Global Perspective," 8.

29. Scherger, "Social Change," 106–29.

Whereas primary institutions work by applying direct control and sanctions, secondary institutions do so to a much lesser extent. Instead, they exert an indirect control, which offers some leeway and sets incentives rather than direct sanctions. In these institutions, individuals mostly have more choice than they had before, but they also *must* choose and *are regarded as responsible for what they choose, even if they do not choose actively.* This imposes new constraints. Furthermore, different actors have different amounts of (material, cognitive, psychological and other) resources at their disposal for dealing with these choices competently. In some cases, the marginal position of actors does not leave them any choice.[30]

Scherger poignantly identifies what I believe is a major flaw in much that has been written on young adults in the United States as of late. The news, media, and even research (until very recently) has identified young adulthood as a period that assumes young adults have chosen the trends that we see among them. Assigning young adults responsibility for these trends gives the impression that they are on an "odyssey of self-exploration," during which they spend ample time exploring who they are, what they believe, and who they might become, while relying on substantial resources from their parents—including living in their parents' home and taking international trips.[31] This extended odyssey is additionally aided by birth control, delay in marriage, and an increase in the number of years spent in higher education. It is increasingly clear that to interpret these trends without giving attention to the grim job market and economic landscape is to ignore some of the secondary institutions that are exerting significant economic and social forces on the lives of young adults, who are bearing the burden of explaining their life situation regardless of the amount of control they had in getting there.

When asked to explain the delay in marriage, Arnett found that young adults reported that "postponing marriage gives you time to grow up, experience life, and 'be happy with yourself.'"[32] While this explanation may have resounded in Arnett's research, which was conducted between 1992 and 2004, the 2010 census report clearly links more negative factors, such as unemployment and job insecurity, with delays in marriage.[33]

30. Scherger, "Social Change," 111. Emphasis mine.

31. Brooks, "The Odyssey Years."

32. Arnett, *Emerging Adulthood*, 101.

33. Arnett, *Emerging Adulthood*, 24–25; Yen, "Census: Recession Taking Toll on Young Adults."

Key findings of the 2010 census include:

- Employment among young adults ages 16–29 stood at 55.3 percent, down from 67.3 percent in 2000 and the lowest since the end of World War II.

- About 1 in 6 older Americans are now in the labor force—the highest level since the 1960s.

- In the past year, 43 of the 50 largest U.S. metropolitan areas continued to post declines in employment.

- The number of households receiving food stamps swelled by 2 million to 13.6 million, meaning that nearly 1 in 8 receives government aid.

- Homeownership declined for a fourth consecutive year, to 65.4 percent, following a peak of 67.3 percent in 2006.

- Marriages fell to a record low last year of just 51.4 percent among adults 18 and over, compared with 57 percent in 2000.[34]

Employment opportunities for young adults are decreasing due to the delay of retirement and the downsizing of many companies. A recent *New York Times* article, citing research conducted through eHarmony and Match.com, interpreted marital delay more positively, stating that the delay in marriage among young adults is evidence that they take marriage more seriously than their parents—but even with this positive spin, the young adults quoted say that they want to pay down loans and know what they have to offer financially to a marriage before committing.[35] Scherger's research from 2009 found this delay to be in direct relationship to financial stability for Germans, as seems to be the case for young adults in the United States.[36]

The trend of living at home with parents continues to increase for American young adults: "Opting to stay put, roughly 5.9 million Americans [ages] 25–34 last year lived with their parents, an increase of 25 percent from before the recession. Driven by a record 1 in 5 young men who doubled up in households, men are now nearly twice as likely as women to live with their parents."[37] These trends are not merely driven by the whim and caprice of a generation of bohemians seeking self-actualization but are the

34. Yen, "Census: Recession Taking Toll on Young Adults."
35. Rabin, "Put a Ring on It?"
36. Scherger, "Social Change," 115.
37. Yen, "Census: Recession Taking Toll on Young Adults."

realities of the 2008–2009 economic recession, which negatively impacted young adults disproportionately to older adults. Having completed this general overview of societal, governmental, familial, and economic shifts, trends and challenges that have led to the lengthening of young adulthood, I will next look at the faith lives of young adults.

THEME TWO: YOUNG ADULTHOOD, THE LEAST RELIGIOUS TIME OF AN INDIVIDUAL'S LIFE

When multiple reports are viewed it is clear that the description of the faith lives of young adults is wrought with dissonant findings. On the one hand, national studies through the Gallup Poll and the Pew Research Center, as well as sociologists such as Robert Wuthnow, Christian Smith, and Robert Putnam, find that young adults today are less religious and that young adulthood generally is the least religious time of an individual's life.[38] This is found when the measurements of religious affiliation, practices (frequency of Bible reading, church attendance, and prayer, for example) and religious beliefs are used. Some of these studies, as well as others, have *also* found that young adults coming of age at the present time are very interested in matters of spirituality and faith, but not as it has traditionally been linked with institutionalized religion. In this section I will highlight the research that exposes young adulthood as both the least religious time of an individual's life and a time of increased interest in existential thought. The two main sources of this information are the National Study of Youth and Religion, which conducted a longitudinal study, revisiting the same youth through their young adult years, and the Gallup Poll, which has been conducting research on the religious practices of Americans through surveys since the 1970s.

Starting with the latter group, various studies have found that religion tends to become increasingly important as one ages. The Gallup Poll, which asks about attitudes and behaviors, compares generational trends. The following table shows that younger generations are less likely to claim church membership than older generations.

---

38. Pew Forum on Religion and Public Life, *Religion among Millennials*; Wuthnow, *After the Baby Boomers*; Smith and Snell, *Souls in Transition*; Putnam and Campbell, *American Grace*.

Table 1.1 Changes in Church Membership by Subgroup[39]

	1998–2000	2016–2018	Change
Total percentage of US adults	69	52	-17
Age 18–29	63	41	-22
Age 30–49	65	49	-16
Age 50–64	71	56	-15
Age 65+	79	64	-15

This table shows that over an eight-year period, those between the ages of eighteen and twenty-two had the largest change with regard to church membership, a drop of 22 percent. According to the Pew Research Center, the Millennial cohort of young adults is less religious than older Americans and this trend is continuing, and amplified, in the following generation. Millennials report being unaffiliated with any denomination or religious tradition with greater frequency than previous generations at their age.[40] They also attend religious services less often than older Americans.[41]

Smith shows this trend in his research, but his research tracks those moving from youth into young adulthood. Across all denominations, Smith found a decrease in practices that would mark an individual as interested in religion:

> Emerging adults who as teenagers were conservative Protestants, mainline Protestants, or Catholics show the largest decrease in weekly or more frequent religious service attendance, at 31, 31, and 26 percent, respectively. Those who as teenagers were Jewish, mainline Protestant, and Catholic reflect the greatest increase in never attending religious services at 38, 28, and 25 percent, respectively. . . . In sum, there is apparent here *an overall decline in religiousness.*[42]

For mainline Protestants the decrease results in only 12 percent of young adults (this wave of Smith's study included individuals within the age

39. Jones, "US Church Membership Down in Past Two Decades."

40. Pew Research Center, *Millennials*, 92.

41. Pew Research Center, *Millennials*, 92.

42. Smith and Snell, *Souls in Transition*, 117. Emphasis mine. See p. 116 of *Souls in Transition* for a clear table showing trends. Smith has adopted the language of "emerging adult." As explained in previous sections, I have chosen to use the language of young adult; however, it is worthwhile to acknowledge that Smith and I are referring to the same group of individuals.

range of eighteen to twenty-three) attending church weekly or more often.[43] For mainline Protestant young adults, the numbers are up to 38 percent who never attend. The piece of information left out here are those who attend once or twice a month; however, despite this, it is clear that using the scale of church attendance, young adults are less religious than they were in their youth.[44]

Smith's findings on reading Scripture were similar, although less staggering. Mainline Protestants, like others, decreased (but only by 1 percent) to only 5 percent saying they read the Bible at least daily. Mainline Protestants claiming never to read Scripture rose by 17 percent to 59 percent.[45]

Prayer, however, was a bit more complicated to discern. Smith found a 7 percent decrease among mainline Protestants.[46] This resulted in 24 percent of the total claiming to pray daily or more often.[47] In addition, there was an increase from 12 percent to a total of 23 percent who claim to never pray.[48] Smith found that there was actually an increase among mainline Protestants who affirmed that in the previous year they had "practiced religious or spiritual meditation not including prayer."[49] While these practices may not meet Smith's definition of "prayer," consequently identifying them as "religious," I do think they indicate a kind of spiritual seeking and exploration—or, as we will see later, "interest." These numbers increased by 14 percent up to a total of 24 percent of mainline Protestants who participated in these meditative practices.[50] It is unclear what both Smith and those surveyed mean by "prayer."

Regarding religious affiliation, Smith reports that from the first round of data collection (age range of thirteen to seventeen) to the second (eighteen to twenty-three) there is an increase of 13 percent of young adults who select "Not Religious" as opposed to selecting a denomination.[51] Those claiming "Protestant" as their religious affiliation are down

43. Smith and Snell, *Souls in Transition*, 4.

44. Smith and Snell, *Souls in Transition*, 116.

45. Smith and Snell, *Souls in Transition*, 116.

46. Smith and Snell, *Souls in Transition*, 116.

47. Smith and Snell, *Souls in Transition*, 116.

48. Smith and Snell, *Souls in Transition*, 116.

49. Smith and Snell, *Souls in Transition*, 116.

50. Smith and Snell, *Souls in Transition*, 116.

51. Smith and Snell, *Souls in Transition*, 106.

from 53 percent to 46 percent, a decrease of 7 percent.[52] Those selecting "Presbyterian/Reformed" are down to 1.46 percent of young adults, a decrease of 0.59 percent.[53] Mainline Protestants have the lowest retention rate of any group, at 50 percent.[54]

In the five years between the first two waves of the National Study of Youth and Religion, "Between 28 and 50 percent of teenage affiliates of U.S. religious traditions change to a different tradition or become nonreligious by their emerging adult years. . . . The largest movement . . . is to the non-religious category."[55] Whereas mainline Protestants lost 20 percent of teenagers to conservative Protestant denominations, conservative Protestants lost only 10 percent of their teenagers to mainline Protestant denominations in their young adult years.[56] This is not easily explained by assuming that young adults are suddenly becoming more religiously conservative. Smith speculates that "in many—if not most—of these cases, there is little religious transformation or conversion going on; rather, youth with probably mostly the same beliefs and dispositions are merely switching Protestant congregations that shift them into a different category according to this analytical method."[57]

Historically, and into the present, conservative Protestants have been more intentional about funding and resourcing campus ministries. These campus ministries include Cru (formerly Campus Crusade for Christ), Fellowship of Christian Athletes, and a myriad of others that were named in my interviews. In interviews I heard from Presbyterian Church (USA) young adults the longing for some kind of ministry that relates to their more progressive stances on gender, environmental, and racial justice, LGBTQ+ inclusion, and Reformed identity; however, most were unable to find these on campus. Of the thirty PC(USA) people I interviewed, three formed their own ministry groups, some overtly PC(USA), others more

---

52. Smith and Snell, *Souls in Transition*, 104.

53. Smith and Snell, *Souls in Transition*, 107.

54. Smith and Snell, *Souls in Transition*, 109.

55. Smith and Snell, *Souls in Transition*, 109–10.

56. Here I believe Smith is on the right track; however, I think the trend he is seeing has to do with individuals going off to college and participating in campus ministry organizations that are different from the denomination in which they were raised. Smith and Snell, *Souls in Transition*, 110.

57. Smith and Snell, *Souls in Transition*, 110.

generically Christian. This exposes a deep longing for a faithful community during young adulthood.[58]

One additional interesting trend is that one-quarter of those who selected "nonreligious" in their teenage years became some kind of "Christian" by their young adult years.[59] I mention this to highlight that for some the transition away from home—perhaps living with non-familial housemates, new roommates at college, or joining military service—brings exposure to new possibilities for faith that actually take hold. These individuals may hold some element of hope for the mainline Protestant denominations. In an attempt to explain how the mainline Protestants can lose 50 percent of their members while retaining a relatively constant "market share" among Christian groups, of about 10 percent, Smith says,

> Mainline Protestantism is relatively bad at retaining its *own* youth as they transition into emerging adulthood but is also relatively *good* at attracting new emerging adults who grew up in other religious traditions—good enough, in fact, to hold their own over these five years in terms of overall "market share." This is noteworthy because it counters so much of the "bad news" that has been continually reported over the last four decades about mainline Protestant decline.[60]

Essentially, Smith is saying that while mainline Protestants are losing many to the "nonreligious" category, Protestantism is actually quite attractive to those transitioning away from home. We might speculate that this trend may have to do with young adults recognizing the socially liberal values that mainline Protestants hold reflected in the Reformed tradition's practices around service, social justice, and inclusion. Elizabeth Drescher and Jean Twenge both identify socially liberal and environmentally progressive values as important in the religious decision-making of young adults.[61] This trend may also be happening because, more so than other denominations, mainline Protestants have a reputation for critical discernment and discussion around hard topics rather than demanding

---

58. I intend to pursue this phenomenon related to campus ministry in later work. I anticipate finding the kinds of results reported by Smith. In fact, I have already found some evidence of this. For example, the PC(USA) reports seeing a dramatic decrease in the religiosity of their young adults due to a lack of ministry outreach as they transition away from home, often into college.

59. Smith and Snell, *Souls in Transition*, 110.

60. Smith and Snell, *Souls in Transition*, 111.

61. Twenge, *iGen*; Drescher, *Choosing Our Religion*.

conformity to beliefs—skills that some young adults are likely acquiring during their college years. Many of the colleges and universities across the United States trace their history back to mainline Protestant founders, but what about those who are not college bound? Furstenberg shows that higher levels of education correlated with delayed marriage. Those who are highly educated are also more likely than less educated populations to have children after marriage. The disparity becomes pronounced in the opportunities and resources available to their children, which reinforces social stratification by class.[62]

In order to fully understand these disparate trends, further research is needed. Even so, these insights are worth considering because they reveal that in order to understand the faith lives of young adults we must ask for more explanation. Even at this point, it is clear that there is dissonance among the findings being reported from different studies. While there seems to be an overall decrease in "religiousness," a closer look has revealed that for some, young adulthood brings about an increase in faith and an expansion of faith practices—sometimes even new commitments regarding religious affiliation. As we will see as we delve deeper, the lack of "religiousness" does not correlate with a lack of interest in religion. In fact, young adults, in high numbers, report that they are "extremely interested" in religion.

THEME THREE: MANY "NONES" ARE ACTUALLY "SOMES," OR A LACK OF "RELIGIOUSNESS" DOES NOT CORRELATE WITH LACK OF FAITH

While we saw, in the previous section, an overall decline in religiosity according to the measures of religious affiliation, church attendance, Bible reading, and prayer, there is not a corresponding decline in interest in faith among young adults. When asked to report on whether or not they had become more or less religious in the previous two years, Smith found that while the majority (59 percent) of those he surveyed reported that they had stayed about the same, only 17 percent reported becoming less religious and 24 percent claimed to be more religious.[63] Regarding the tension with earlier findings, Smith says, "This may strike one as odd, considering that many of the statistics discussed earlier seem to suggest a modest overall

62. Furstenberg, "Family Change in Global Perspective," 11.

63. Smith and Snell, *Souls in Transition*, 126.

decline in the religious affiliations, importance, practices, and beliefs of emerging adults."[64] Elaborating further, Smith says, "From their own perspectives, most new emerging adults had not changed much religiously in the previous two years, and more reported becoming more religious than less religious."[65] Smith found that "mainline Protestant cases were the most likely to have become less religious."[66] He found that of mainline Protestants 16 percent claimed to have become more religious, 60 percent stayed about the same, and 23 percent became less religious.[67]

Worthy of our attention is the tension between the perceptions that young adults have of themselves as having a general increase in religiosity despite a decline in traditional measures of religiosity. In her 2016 book *Choosing Our Religion: The Spiritual Lives of America's Nones*, Elizabeth Drescher explores this very tension.[68] Drescher complicates the story of those selecting "none" as their religious affiliation—whose growing numbers in national polls have once again sounded the alarm of decline in Christianity. Unlike others who are fearful of the rise of this growing group, Drescher shines light on the Nones, showing that they are not as immoral or irreligious as we may think. She exposes a complicated and thoughtful landscape in a territory that seems newly discovered. The Nones, however, are likely a group that has always existed, but now they have a box to check, and as time passes, more are finding that this is the authentic response they have been wanting to register for some time.

The stories that emerge from Drescher's skillfully conducted interviews provide rare opportunities to listen to candid descriptions of why many Nones are no longer affiliated with religious groups; these range from benign descriptions of drifting away to a heartbreaking story of one pastor trying to "pray the gay away" that ends with a literal slap to the face. While this does not seem to be Drescher's intention, these stories show the real pain that the church has inflicted.

Choosing Our Religion begins by showing how the statistics about Nones can mislead people to assume that all Nones are atheists. Drescher points out that many Nones are actually "Somes" (they have some religious beliefs). From this starting point, Drescher shows that there seem to be

---

64. Smith and Snell, *Souls in Transition*, 126.

65. Smith and Snell, *Souls in Transition*, 126.

66. Smith and Snell, *Souls in Transition*, 127.

67. Smith and Snell, *Souls in Transition*, 126.

68. Drescher, *Choosing Our Religion*.

some trends among Nones regarding their departure from specific Christian groups. Those who have left mainline Protestant denominations often have less emotionally charged reasons for leaving than some Evangelicals, who feel they have been lied to (regarding the age of the earth, for example).

Drescher's previous work concerns social networking. Drawing on Pierre Bourdieu's claim that individuals distinguish themselves by their taste, Drescher shows how the Internet helps Nones find one another based on common spiritual "taste" in an author, a cause, or a practice—providing affiliation for the unaffiliated.

For those assuming Nones are atheistic nihilists, Drescher provides convincing evidence from interviews and "the numbers" that 40 percent of Nones pray and have a strong moral impulse to care for others. Nones additionally have a strong moral compass, as is evident in their frequent references to the Golden Rule, the story of the Good Samaritan, and their admiration of Jesus as a moral exemplar. In addition to naming the stories and practices that the Nones have appropriated from Christianity, Drescher exposes the frustration many Nones have with the hypocrisy of some Christians and the bad, unloving theology they profess. While many Nones seem to use Christian resources for their spiritual practices and ethical views, there are also some who are more intentional in distancing themselves from Christianity while maintaining very thoughtful spiritual and ethical practices.

Ultimately, Drescher suggests that Nones are actually quite religious and often use the resources that many religious institutions provide. She suggests that rather than trying to win them back or seek their conversion to membership, Christians might instead try to engage them through listening to their stories and questions and inviting them into shared acts of mercy and justice.[69]

As Drescher shows, for young adults, the religious life seems to include much more than has been traditionally been measured. Additionally, quantitative studies tend to highlight those who are in the majority, masking trends among those in the minority. Listening to the individual stories of young adults (as Drescher did through qualitative interviews) exposes new themes among young adult faith.

Those in their young adult years are not giving great amounts of money to congregations, but as we will see below, they do have a robust

69. Parts of the above section come from my review of Elizabeth Drescher's *Choosing Our Religion*, published in *Theology Today* 74 (2017).

understanding of using one's God-given gifts. They do not necessarily take time to sit down every day and read their Bibles—although some do—but they do read fantasy books and poetry that open up their imagination to the possible qualities of God. They do not regularly attend church, but they are intentional in their seeking of divine encounter in nature or in social gatherings. They are eager to talk about matters of faith and spirituality to those who reach out to them—and they claim to meet God beyond the walls of the church. They also participate in many focusing or meditative practices such as journaling, dancing, yoga, or listening to music, which function devotionally as a time of prayer for them but may not lead them to check the "prayer" box on a survey.

THEME FOUR: AESTHETIC ATTUNEMENT IS GREATER FOR THIS COHORT

Aesthetic Interest Generally

Young adulthood is a time of freedom and creativity where some individuals engage the arts as a medium for discernment, existential wondering, and divine encounter. For Millenials this is especially true, in part because their school-age years coincided with the largest amount of funding for the arts in public school education in the history of the National Endowment for the Arts (NEA).[70] According to Wuthnow, this cohort of young adults is "more likely than older adults to have taken art and music classes in school or to have received private lessons in ballet or creative writing."[71] As cuts to the budget of the NEA continue, this cohort will likely have had more arts education than the generations who follow as well. In addition to having more arts education generally, young adults "point to art and music as

---

70. Osborne shows the link between political ideologies in the United States with funding for the arts through the NEA, which was established in 1965 by Lyndon B. Johnson. Ronald Reagan, Newt Gingrich, and Donald Trump have all proposed cutting the NEA altogether but were never able to successfully eliminate it. The NEA reached its peak of $160–180 million dollars per year of funding from the mid-1980s to the mid-1990s when the cohort of young adults interviewed for this study were in elementary, middle and high school. Funding was cut in 1996 to $99 million. Since 2004, funding has steadily increased from $144 million to $167.5 million in 2010; however, it was cut to $154 million in 2011, and as of 2018 the budget is $152 million. It is not coincidental that these trends have seen their most significant shifts during the first years of a new presidency. Osborne, "Marketplace of Ideas."

71. Wuthnow, *After the Baby Boomers*, 47.

sources of inspiration. When creeds and doctrines fail them, they turn to the more intuitive lessons from the arts."[72] Wuthnow emphasizes that while the arts may seem to play only an "entertainment" role for young adults, this is not the case—art and music are "a very important part of their lives . . . and is one that we will see interacting with their faith as well."[73]

In his 2004 work, Richard Florida also noted the significance of creative engagement among young adults and called this "the rise of the creative class." Florida noted how this generation was entering a workforce where their creative impulses would help them lead and thrive.[74] There is no shortage of secular evidence to demonstrate that this is happening. Students are lined up to learn Design Thinking at Stanford University, which engages in empathetic listening to move into creative action (experimentation). Websites like Etsy.com combine the opportunity to support individual and "local" artists (making the economic choice not to support mass industry) with the environmentally friendly choice to have greater ability to question and filter the kinds of materials in products.[75] This is the generation who went through hours of lessons in elementary school singing the refrain "Reduce, Recycle, Reuse." Now that this generation has come of age, many have incorporated this ethical choice into their aesthetic choices—choosing "upcycled" items to decorate their homes, such as reclaimed wooden kitchen tables or recycled T-shirt rugs.[76]

This aesthetic interest is not limited to consumerism but is also something people simply enjoy because it brings meaning to their lives. This is apparent in the "Make" movement, where men gather to share what they have made from upcycled (often technological or mechanical) products.[77] Faythe Levine and Courtney Heimerl made a documentary (which has also taken form as a book) to capture the art and craft movement

72. Wuthnow, *After the Baby Boomers*, 48.

73. Wuthnow, *After the Baby Boomers*, 47.

74. Florida, *The Rise of the Creative Class*.

75. Etsy.com has art ranging from professional-level paintings to clothing and jewelry to art created by young (children) entrepreneurs.

76. The term "upcycle" is a play on the word "recycle." Unlike recycling, those who upcycle repurpose used items such as fabric, wood, and beads to create new products. For example, Paul Kind has started a company where they use reclaimed wood to build furniture: see www.arborla.com.

77. *Makezine* is an online magazine that shares information about "Make": http://makezine.com/.

as it has been embodied among this generation of young women.[78] The DIY (do-it-yourself) ethos has been embraced by many young adults who enjoy spending time gardening, canning and preserving food, fermenting kombucha and beer, building IKEA furniture, or making cheese despite the fact that it is more time-consuming and expensive than simply buying it from a grocery (or furniture) store.

An older man doing woodworking and a grandmother crocheting a baby blanket are not new trends. Perhaps what is surprising about these trends is that they are, in a sense, being "upcycled" or reclaimed—not out of necessity but for the joy of the "making" process—by a young generation choosing to make time for these activities that align with their values, which include resistance to traditional consumerist culture. In the 1960s Rose Wilder Lane, daughter of Laura Ingalls Wilder, explained the political, economic, and social dimensions of "making" by nonprofessional artists. I believe her comments about needlework and women may be applied to the aesthetic activity of this cohort of young adults today:

> Needlework is the art that tells the truth about the real life of people in their time and place. The great arts, music, sculpture, painting, literature, are the work of a few unique persons whom lesser men emulate, often for generations. Needlework is anonymous; the people create it. Each piece is the work of a woman who is thinking only of making for her child, her friend, her home or herself a thing of beauty that pleases her.
>
> So her needlework expresses what she is, more clearly than her handwriting does. It expresses everything that makes her an individual unlike any other person—her character, her mind and her spirit, her experience in living. It expresses, too, her country's history and culture, the traditions, the philosophy, the way of living that she takes for granted.[79]

It seems that aesthetic or artistic participation is no longer only for starving artists or those with copious amounts of time and money on their hands (if it ever was). Crafts, music, and art are also not made merely for utility; rather, artistic activity is for the average person because there is something worthwhile in the doing and making process.[80] To make something is to

78. Levine and Heimerl, *Handmade Nation: The Rise of DIY, Art, Craft, and Design.*

79. Lane, *Woman's Day Book of American Needlework*, 10.

80. English distinguishes between "to do" and "to make"; however, that distinction is not always present in other languages. In German, for example, the word *machen* can mean "to do," "to make," "to create," or "to render."

"tell the truth about the real life of people in their time and place." There is a timelessness to Wilder's insightful words from the 1960s. If Wilder is right that this kind of anonymous art "expresses everything that makes her [or him] an individual unlike any other person—her character, her mind and her spirit, her experience in living," then it is not surprising that those going through young adulthood—and discerning their identity—would be inclined to participate in the arts.

Aesthetic Attentiveness in Faith

It is significant to note that there is also increasing interest in aesthetic practices in congregations, especially as they promote vibrancy within congregations. In his book *Congregations in America*, sociologist Mark Chaves includes an entire chapter on the arts, emphasizing their significance for religion and religious practices. Again, we might ask, is this really new, or is it a persistent desire within humanity to participate in the aesthetic richness of making? Chaves argues against distinguishing between high and low art. This distinction is interesting because the DIY movement, Etsy.com, and "Make" are all examples of the blurring of the lines between high and low art. Chaves writes,

> If we expand the concept of art to include popular practices as well as high culture, reserve judgment about artistic quality, and resist the temptation to oppose kitschy popular culture to "real" art, then art and religion seem much less opposed. Stated more positively, if we conceptualize artistic practice broadly as the making or consuming of music, dance, drama, and objects for display, without respect to the venue in which they are practiced or displayed, the skill with which they are executed or constructed, the audience to which they are primarily addressed, the overall quality of the product, or whether these practices are pursued as ends in themselves—art for art's sake—rather than as means to some other end, then connections between the arts and religion, especially religion as it is practiced in congregations, becomes more clear.[81]

Essentially, Chaves seems to be saying that if we start to look at the value of participating in art—either as a "maker" or "consumer"—then we can begin to see the connection that the arts naturally have with religion and religious practice.

81. Chaves, *Congregations in America*, 168.

Chaves highlights the "bridging" and "bonding" effects of the arts, two categories he gleans from Robert Putnam.[82] The arts function to bridge relationships between the congregation and outside community. The arts also function to bond individuals within congregations together. Choirs are excellent examples of both. Professional musicians or singers may be brought into the congregation or choirs may sing outside of the congregation in the act of bridging. Choirs also bond individuals together as they rehearse and lead worship together. While these are significant insights into the role that aesthetic participation plays in congregations, they fail to ask how individuals are affected, particularly as this participation relates to the faith lives of individuals. What I believe is most helpful to glean from Chaves is his explicit claim that congregations are places where individuals have substantial and significant exposure to art that functions in these bridging and bonding ways. "The arts," he writes, "are used to produce religion, and religion provides social and organizational contexts for artistic activity."[83]

Similar trends connecting aesthetic attention and congregational vibrancy were found by Robert Wuthnow in his work *All in Sync: How Music and Art Are Revitalizing American Religion*.[84] Wuthnow does not seek to claim that the arts are the only influence generating interest in spirituality; however, he does claim that they have a significant impact. Wuthnow found that the arts can act as a bridge to faith, and vice versa. Paying attention not only to current practices but also to formative events happening over a lifetime, he writes,

> The connections between spirituality and artistic interests are, for the most part, taking place among ordinary people. In many cases, a childhood interest in spirituality is later encouraged by learning a form of artistic expression; in others, early participation in the arts leads to a later interest in spirituality.[85]

Again, art is no longer for the wealthy, for those with extensive leisure time, or for those willing to be starving artists, but rather for "ordinary people." Like Wuthnow, I found that childhood participation in art establishes a connection with spirituality early in life that influences faith expression and participation later on. Wuthnow claims that if his findings are true—that artistic interest can lead to an increase in spiritual expression and promote

82. Chaves, *Congregations in America*, 169–70.

83. Chaves, *Congregations in America*, 170.

84. Wuthnow, *All in Sync*.

85. Wuthnow, *All in Sync*, 16.

greater involvement in faith communities—there are wide-ranging impli-cations for religious leaders.[86] This claim is especially important to reflect on regarding the religious participation of young adults, who, as we have seen, are less active than any other age group in congregational life.

Aesthetic Attunement for Faith in Young Adults

Like Chaves, sociologists Richard Flory and Donald Miller consider the role of the arts in congregations, but they look specifically at young adults. In their book *Finding Faith: The Spiritual Quest of the Post-Boomer Generation*, they categorize young adults as Innovators, Appropriators, Resisters, and Re-claimers.[87] Despite differences in their relationships to tradition and culture, which are revealed by the names they have chosen to label the different groups, Flory and Miller found that all young adults embrace an embodied spirituality that is expressed through the aesthetic choices made for their worship space and practice.[88] The spectrum ranges from "Innovators and Reclaimers, who embrace the body, community and experience, to Appropriators, who seek personal identity, expression, and experience that imitates much that is available to the larger culture, and Resisters, who work hard to deny the body and experience, and seek to create their own sense of community through their insistence on rationality, logic, and cognitive pursuits."[89]

According to Flory and Miller, aesthetic awareness in relationship to faith practices informs the religious practice of young adults. We may speculate as to the cause of this (arts education in public schools, the influence of Howard Gardner's "Multiple Intelligence" theory on public and Christian education, greater access to the arts through the Internet), but important to note is that there is consensus among researchers that young adults seek to participate in religious practices that are aesthetically embodied.[90] Bodily awareness, attention to the expression of personal identity, and a focus on experience are all markers of the faith lives of young adults—especially when they connect an individual to the community:

86. Wuthnow, *All in Sync*, 17.

87. Flory and Miller, *Finding Faith*.

88. Flory and Miller, *Finding Faith*, 168.

89. Flory and Miller, *Finding Faith*, 168.

90. Gardner, *Frames of Mind*.

Whether it is through the stained glass, icons, and incense of the liturgical traditions, or the creation of various artworks intended to express their particular spiritual experience, or service to others, these only have personal meaning within the context of the religious community. These young people are not the spiritual consumers of their parents' generation. Rather, they are seeking both a deep spiritual experience and a community experience, each of which provides them with meaning in their lives, and each of which is meaningless without the other.[91]

Young adults are interested in not only the communal connections made possible through congregational involvement but also the potential to encounter God and have a "spiritual experience" as well as express their faith. They want to bodily participate in the community. The mantra for Burning Man, the popular gathering that attracts thousands of young adults to Nevada every summer, provides a neat summary: "Don't spectate, participate."[92] Participation is very important for young adults and will only grow in importance as social media and online media create more opportunities for nearly constant virtual participation.[93] Flory and Miller call this "expressive communalism" and conclude that it is common among all religious young adults. Young adults have embedded their lives in spiritual communities in which their desire and need for both expressive and experiential activities, whether through art, music, or service, and for a close-knit, physical community and communion with others are met.[94] Flory and Miller conclude by encouraging congregations to embrace the "embodied imaginations" of young adults in order to "ensure for themselves a vibrant future."[95]

CONCLUSION

In this chapter I have argued that young adulthood is a time when interest in matters of faith and spirituality are increasing despite the lack of religiosity according to traditional measures. Using Chaves and Wuthnow, I have highlighted the reality that the arts are playing a significant role

91. Flory and Miller, *Finding Faith*, 188.
92. See "You Are Burning Man," available at http://www.burningman.com.
93. Jenkins, *Confronting the Challenges of Participatory Culture*.
94. Flory and Miller, *Finding Faith*, 189.
95. Flory and Miller, *Finding Faith*, 189.

in the communal life of congregations. As we have seen in the research of Flory and Miller, young adults are especially interested in aesthetically rich, embodied religious experiences. Having reviewed the major sociological studies that report on the arts and faith, as well as the faith of young adults, I now turn to my own research study. This research sought to answer the question, What role do the arts play in the faith lives of young adults? For a few—two out of thirty—the arts played no role at all in their faith life; despite this, all but one said that the arts were important in some way in their faith lives.

In the next chapter, I will share findings from my research through personal, one-on-one interviews with thirty young adults who were at one time or another connected with the Presbyterian Church (USA). Some of what they shared will reinforce the findings presented in this chapter; however, some of what I found challenges or offers more nuanced interpretations on research with young adults.

2

ART CONNECTS, EXPRESSES, AND OPENS

In this chapter I report the findings of my 2011 research project on the faith practices of Presbyterian Church (USA) young adults, specifically with regard to the role of the arts. I propose that the arts function in the faith lives of young adults in three ways: by aiding young adults in *connecting* with others and God, by assisting in the *expression* of faith and identity, and by serving as a medium through which young adults are *opened up* to new interpretations of God. These findings will be analyzed through the lens of aesthetic learning theory in chapter 3 to claim that participation in the arts functions as aesthetic practical reason, facilitating Christian identity formation and transformation as young adults go through this phase of life. In chapter 5 I analyze my findings through the lens of the Reformed tradition to claim that the arts carry a unique power to form individuals, a power that has historically been feared within the church. I will argue that this power should not be feared but embraced.

OVERVIEW OF METHODS

I conducted thirty-four interviews between March and October of 2011. Of these thirty-four, only thirty fit within the limited scope of this research, which was defined as including young adults who were between the ages of eighteen and thirty and who were presently or formerly active within a

PC(USA) congregation. The extra four interviews were conducted with individuals who did not fit into these categories—they were a year or two outside of the age range, or they were not affiliated with the PC(USA) but were excited about the project and did not tell me that they did not meet these criteria until we were well into the interview. Participants were selected through snowball sampling or through a preliminary online survey that I conducted about faith and the arts and that was distributed through social media in the fall of 2010. All research participants took the online survey, which allowed me to compare their responses to closed-ended questions. The interviews were conducted in person or over Skype and, in two instances, over the phone.[1] They ranged in length from a half hour to two hours.

All of those interviewed were American citizens. They lived in twelve different states and three countries other than the US; one moved back to the US the day before our interview. They called fifteen different states home, all within the lower 48. Of those living in the US at the time, most resided in the Northeast and Midwest.

I will engage these interviews in a way that exposes the role that the arts play in the faith lives of young adults so that the church, as a body, might gain insight and respond accordingly. The general response of those interviewed to the question, "What role does participation in the arts play in your faith life?" was that the arts provide opportunities for connection, expression, and opening.[2] These three themes will be further elaborated below.

Age and Mobility

The average age of those interviewed was 23.4 and the median age was 23.5. We did not discuss their age during the interview; however, I was interested in their self-perceptions surrounding their age.[3] In order to discover their psychological age I asked two questions through the survey. The first asked young adults to select the category they felt best described their current life stage: Youth, Young Adult, Emerging Adult, or Adult. Less than 1 percent

1. Skype is software that provides a telephone and video service through the Internet. Skype was used for interviews, rather than phone calls, due to the ease of audio recording and the possibility of viewing one another over video. In total fifteen interviews were conducted over Skype, thirteen were conducted in person, and two were conducted over the phone because the individual was on a road trip.

2. Richard R. Osmer helped me to see these three themes within the interviews.

3. See Appendix C for a chart showing the age distribution of research participants.

selected Youth, with a fairly even distribution among the other three categories. The second open-ended question regarding psychological age was, "What factors or events in your life led you to select the category you chose in [the previous] question?" The trend among the thirty interviewed was to comment primarily on the following:

- *finances* and their dependence or independence from parents or grandparents;
- *career* or status as a student.

Secondarily they commented on

- *marriage* as a marker for adulthood;
- *feeling* as though they fit into one category as opposed to another;
- *living situation*, especially regarding distance from home or paying their own rent and bills.

For those who checked "Adult" a typical answer was, "I'm married, finishing my master's degree and earn 100 percent of my own income." One who selected "Emerging Adult" wrote,

> I am still trying to determine how to best use my interests, gifts, and talents. I'm thinking of going back to grad school. I feel I have more growing, or "emerging," to do, although I consider myself mature and responsible.

One who checked "Young Adult" described her reason for selecting it as

> Nothing in particular. Having lived on my own for a couple of years, I feel like a capable and independent individual. However, given that I live with roommates and am in school full-time, I don't necessarily feel as though I've achieved full adulthood. I think that the continuation of my education is the main thing there—this schoolwork is the last specific thing I want to set in place in order to start myself on a particular career track, and while I enjoyed my past jobs, I really felt as though they were something I was doing to allow myself a breather before going back to school.

The differences between the answers of individuals who checked "Young Adult" and the answers of those who checked "Emerging Adult" were minimal. If anything, as in the first quote above, those who selected the box "Emerging Adult" sometimes did so because they were drawn to the notion of "emerging" or going through a process. This indicates to me that the category of "emerging adulthood" is meaningful for those research-ing young adults but has yet to become common parlance among young adults themselves.

Regarding geography and mobility, I asked the young adults in this study to list the number of places they have lived in the last five years. The mean number of moves was 5.5, while the average was three. The most anyone moved was eleven times and the least was none (totaling "one" residence). This confirms and gives greater detail to Arnett's finding that the high mobility of young adults contributes to the feeling of being "in between."[4] It also shows, however, that there are individuals who are not highly mobile. About 14 percent of the young adults that I surveyed did not report moving at all in the last five years. Thirty percent had lived in only two places, moving only once.[5] While Arnett is correct to point out that young adulthood is the most highly mobile time of life, this does not seem to be the case for every young adult, which may be explained in a number of ways. One explanation is that today's young adults, in higher numbers than young adults of previous generations, are continuing to live at home with their parents to save money. Living at home also seems to be correlated with delay of marriage. The low numbers also may represent those in their early twenties who, unlike those in their late twenties, have not yet had the opportunity to move.[6]

GENERAL OVERVIEW OF INTERVIEW FINDINGS

It is clear from the previous chapter that young adults value the arts, but in order to answer *why* this is the case and *how* the arts function in their faith lives we must rely on qualitative findings gathered through interviews. In his recent article "Taking Talk Seriously: Religious Discourse as Social Practice," sociologist Robert Wuthnow challenges those using qualitative methods of research to treat the "talk" happening in interviews as a unique

---

4. Arnett, *Emerging Adulthood*, 11–12.

5. This data has not been run through multiple regression analysis, which could potentially show a correlation between age and the number of times an individual has moved in the last five years.

6. Running a cross tabulation with respect to age and number of places lived would expose this data. For the purposes of this research study, however, it is sufficient to note that while young adults are generally "highly mobile," this is not the case for all young adults.

resource for insight and depth of meaning.[7] Wuthnow traces the historical trajectory of the reputation of interview-based research through the 1960s, 1970s, and 1980s, leading to the academic acceptance of interviews as a legitimate vehicle for doing research. Despite the general acceptance, however, Wuthnow points out that interviews are often still used as anecdotes to quantitative research or are analyzed quantitatively despite their qualitative nature (e.g., "75 percent of those interviewed claimed to dislike contemporary worship music").

As an alternative, Wuthnow considers how qualitative researchers might continue the tradition of Bourdieu, Foucault, Burke, and Swidler, who "proposed that culture not be thought of as underlying beliefs and values influencing behavior, but as a toolkit of habits, skills, and styles from which people conduct strategies of action."[8] To this end, Wuthnow proposes that qualitative researchers give greater attention to patterns of speech and the scripted forms within the narrative context that surround an issue. To emphasize this Wuthnow says,

> Talk is cultural work that people *do* to make sense of their lives and to orient their behavior. It is a toolkit—culture in action, in Swidler's terms—with which to do work, but it is more than an after the fact justification. It serves rather as the means through which values and beliefs acquire sufficient meaning to guide behavior and to provide a template for self-understanding.[9]

It is with this definition of the function of "talk" in mind that I interpret the findings from my research. The following interpretation of my findings regarding contemporary versus traditional music illustrates how I have implemented Wuthnow's insights.

While interviewing young adults to discover the role that the arts play in their faith lives, I found many who raised the recent church debate between contemporary and traditional music—despite the fact that I never directly asked about contemporary or traditional music. With increasing frequency, I noticed that the responses of the majority seemed to follow a common pattern. Our discourse would follow a pattern somewhat like this: I would ask a scripted question (I asked ten questions in total, and their comments on music came in response to almost any of the

7. Wuthnow, "Taking Talk Seriously," 1–21.

8. Wuthnow, "Taking Talk Seriously," 4.

9. Wuthnow, "Taking Talk Seriously," 9; emphasis mine.

questions), and they would say something like the following, the response of a young man named Drew:

> I know a lot of young people find that stuff [contemporary music] great and find it really engaging for them, but I have the exact op-posite reaction. To me it is a lot of noise and it's a lot of sound and fury and it's not expressing more content, and I don't think it is ex-pressing content in a new and interesting way. I think if anything it dilutes the message. The message becomes whatever medium they are using. And much less, this is a new way to think about God, this is a new way to challenge your relationship, so I don't know if the stuff you have been doing is related to this question of what is the role of contemporary music in churches, but for my part I find it a distraction to worship more than anything else.[10]

Another young man, Sam, said, "I'm very happy with the way we do music in the church with hymns and stuff. I wouldn't want to say, 'more contemporary services' or what have you."[11] Susan confirmed this as well as stating that she felt like an exception:

> Maybe it might just be strange for me being a twenty-three-year-old to be so connected to old church music, because I feel like a lot of young people like the contemporary services and they like the new Christian music. But I tend to prefer the old hymns that are 200 to 250 years old because it seems much more religious to me, because it is not quite the usual. And also . . . Taizé music is an incredibly religious experience to me; repetition and chanting the time of year during Lent has always been special to me and I really enjoy that.[12]

Unlike most of her peers, Jennifer assumed that I had been hearing that many young adults actually prefer traditional music. She explained her preference for traditional music in this way:

> I mean, it's probably a lot of what you have already heard, and I think the word is getting out there that young adults don't neces-sarily want contemporary, that they assume that the casual dress and the praise team is inviting and friendly, but I think at least for

10. Drew, interview by Katherine M. Douglass, transcript, April 2011. All interviews were conducted in confidentiality, and the names of interviewees have been changed by mutual agreement except where noted. Transcripts of all interviews are available upon request.

11. Sam, interview by Katherine M. Douglass, transcript, July 2011.

12. Susan, interview by Katherine M. Douglass, transcript, September 2011.

myself I want something that is more thoughtful. I mean, I can put my iPod on and play music that makes me feel good—I don't need to go to church for that. Challenge me, nourish me, and give me something that is more than the sticker on my Sunday passport.[13]

Sam was similarly aware of the incorrect assumption that young adults prefer contemporary music. "I know most of the younger generation at the church [I attend] liked the regular service with hymns and most of them would rather have that, and I'd rather have that too," he said.[14] It is likely that being affiliated with the PC(USA), either now or in their childhood, has something to do with shaping these "traditional" tastes and preferences for what feels like authentic worship.

There were a few exceptions to this, including one young woman whose explanation seems to echo what I have heard in many conversations about reaching out to young adults. Answering a question about what churches could do to reach out to young adults, Emily said, "I guess I would say, really use the arts to reach out, like I said using the contemporary music during the service or something like that will help to draw more young people in."[15] She assumed a correlation between young people and contemporary music—a consistent assumption among the majority of young adults whom I interviewed. This is a perception young adults have about other young adults despite their own preferences for traditional or more liturgical worship. According to their own answers, this appears to be a huge misconception that is influencing evangelistic and outreach efforts—at least among those in the PC(USA).

For the few who preferred contemporary music, it was clear that this arose from their experience of playing in a praise band that played contemporary music or through exposure to contemporary music while attending a camp during their youth. For example, Sean said, "I started playing the guitar for contemporary worship in high school, and I have been doing it ever since."[16] This resonates with Henry Jenkins' claim in *Confronting the Challenges of Participatory Culture* that young adults of the current generation place a high value on participation.[17] Regarding

---

13. Jennifer, interview by Katherine M. Douglass, transcript, September 2011.

14. Sam, interview.

15. Emily, interview by Katherine M. Douglass, transcript, July 2011.

16. Sean, interview by Katherine M. Douglass, transcript, July 2011.

17. Jenkins, *Confronting the Challenges of Participatory Culture*.

musical tastes for worship, it seems that participating in the creation of music trumps personal preference.[18]

While many articulated an appreciation for contemporary music and the fact that it theoretically reaches a broader audience, on a weekly basis the majority of young adults I interviewed prefer to sing traditional music in the form of hymns, songs from Taizé, or international songs. Margot's comment sums up the common sentiment of most of the young adults that I interviewed: "I like contemporary music outside of the church context, but it seems more church-y to me with traditional hymns in the service."[19]

Wuthnow would draw our attention to the pattern of speech that each of these individuals followed. Why is it that so many took an apologetic tone? Why did each assume they were exceptional when they were actually the majority? Perhaps this is because they have heard that the Presbyterian denomination is declining in membership and that, in an effort to reach out to their demographic, great attempts to be more relevant through contemporary music have been made (somewhat unsuccessfully).[20] Perhaps these individuals were comparing themselves and their worship preferences to their perceptions of young adults generally (across the entire United States) rather than within their own denomination.[21]

18. There are potentially more factors at play here. To follow up on this topic I would want to ask young adults about how their participation made them feel as though they belonged. This is highlighted somewhat under the category of "Connecting" later on in this chapter, although not specifically with regard to the contemporary versus traditional music discussion.

Regarding the participatory culture explicitly, this seems to be a matter of participation versus passivity rather than taste. This is potentially pointing out that there is a deeper human need that worship addresses such as belonging, participation, and meaning-making. These human needs are deeper than taste, which reveals consumer rather than participatory motives. Thank you to Kenda Dean for these insights, which will be further addressed in the fifth chapter.

19. Margot, interview by Katherine M. Douglass, transcript, July 2011.

20. From conversations I have had with pastors it seems that contemporary services in PC(USA) congregations tend to attract those in their forties and fifties rather than young adults. Oftentimes, it seems that it is those who are in their forties and fifties serving on the worship committee and making decisions about worship style. As Susan said, "So what do you think it is? Forty- to forty-five-year-old people deciding that they will get young people to church by playing contemporary music?" Susan, interview.

21. In his recent work, *American Grace*, Robert Putnam would likely explain this as a predictable response among mainline young adults to an increasingly vocal religious right. Putnam and Campbell, *American Grace*.

As Drew said, the added "sound and fury" of contemporary music do not "express more content," but rather distract from a more sincere expression of faith.[22] Regarding connection, Susan said that singing songs from Taizé or songs that are 200 to 250 years old aid her in feeling connected with the historic and international church.[23] She also mentioned Lent, exposing her awareness and value of liturgical seasons, which are often ignored in more contemporary patterns for worship.[24]

Shifting away from the debate over traditional and contemporary music, the most pronounced pattern I found throughout the interviews answered the question I initially posed for my research: "What role does participation in the arts play in the faith lives of young adults?" Those interviewed consistently responded throughout the interviews that the arts function to provide opportunities for connection, expression, and opening—to God and others (the quotes above highlight the connecting and expressing quality of music). This language pattern—connecting, expressing, opening—is threaded throughout these young adults' answers to a variety of questions. Attending to this pattern has revealed the function that the arts play in the faith lives of young adults. Analyzing this "talk" reveals more than a simple confirmation of quantitative studies—yes, they do use the words "express," "connect," and "open" frequently. It additionally exposes the role that the arts are playing in the faith lives of young adults—the value of the arts lies in the way that they aid expression, connection, and opening.

The challenge, as Wuthnow points out, is to sit with our transcriptions and audio recordings long enough to begin to hear and reflect on the self-understanding that individuals come to as they expose what they find meaningful in the articulation of their values and beliefs. The challenge is also to resist the temptation of going to one of two extremes—either to engage these findings only as confirmations or anecdotes to quantitative research or to claim to be exposing the unconscious motivations of those interviewed.

SPECIFIC INTERVIEW FINDINGS

The reporting of findings will be limited in scope, focusing on findings from my primary research question: "What role do the arts play in the

22. Drew, interview.

23. Susan, interview.

24. Susan, interview.

faith lives of young adults?" Going into this research my hunch was that the arts play a significant role in the devotional practices of young adults as well as functioning as one of the ways they express their faith and "make meaning" in their lives.[25]

Three main themes became apparent. First, the arts aid in helping individuals *connect* both to one another and to God. Second, the arts provide a tool or avenue through which young adults *express* their faith and identity by communicating (in word, sound, or symbol) their struggles and beliefs. Third, the arts serve as a catalyst to *open* perspectives, worldviews, and relationships. What is exciting about these findings is that they expose *how* the arts are functioning. The arts are not merely something these young adults passively encounter and "like"—the arts function to actively connect people, express identity, and open up new avenues for knowing. These three functions of art also pose a challenging question to congregations: Within the life of a congregation, where do individuals have opportunities for expressing their faith and identity, connecting with others, and opening up to new perspectives or encounters with God?

There are two caveats I must add before exploring these three themes. First, while these findings were true for most of the young adults I interviewed, they were not true for all of them. As I mentioned above, whereas for some, participation in the arts is central to their faith, for others there is no connection, and for one individual the arts were not at all important (in relationship to his faith or otherwise). It should be noted, therefore, that the arts function to *connect, express,* and *open* for those who find encounters with art meaningful—for this study, that was twenty-nine out of thirty, but not everyone.

The second caveat is that for those who continue to claim Christianity as their faith, the arts have not taken a primary place, but rather enhance and deepen their worship, devotional practices, and relationships with others and God.[26] As Mary explained, "I think it supplements my

25. I came to this hypothesis through my own interactions with and observations of young adults, as well as various literature and movements among this generation of young adults that mark them as an especially creative cohort. Popular and academic works have identified similar trends. For further reading on this topic, see McCracken, *Hipster Christianity*; Flory and Miller, *Finding Faith*; Levine and Heimerl, *Handmade Nation*; and Merritt, *Tribal Church*.

26. It should also be noted that two of those interviewed now consider themselves to be atheist or agnostic. Both were raised in the church, and one became involved in a congregation because of the strong music program. Of these two individuals, both continue to find the arts to be a medium through which they make sense of the world, but not

devotional life. I wouldn't say it is necessary for my devotional life, but it's something that I do that adds to my life that I do in a similar way. It brings me that same sort of peace where I can basically not focus on the trivial things that weigh me down, but actually focus on the things that are important."[27] Similarly, Erin said, "It is definitely not a primary role—it is not in the background—but it is not the first thing that comes to mind in terms of my faith."[28] In other words, if we were to take away all of the color, music, dance, poetry, and prose from their lives, they would still believe—but if we were to ask (and we are), then yes, the arts do play an important role in their faith lives. All but one differentiated these areas of their life when they discussed them. The arts play an enriching and deepening role without being confused or conflated to the point of being idolatrous—meaning that they did not consider art to be something to be worshiped, but rather something that aids in their worship and devotion of God. Only one young man whom I interviewed bordered on conflating the arts and religion. His initial comments seem to indicate that he saw a difference between participating in the arts and practicing faith. For example, John said, "I think there might be some connection to the state of mind you are in when you are making art and when you are in spiritual worship."[29] However, as we talked it became clear that he saw the two as essentially the same. When I interviewed him, John was fasting to practice Ramadan with his Muslim friends as well as reading from a variety of Christian mystics. His operative theological view was of "One God" and he told me that he tried to live as though all religions were true. Additionally, he went to great lengths to resist the division between the spiritual and physical world. In his words, "The spiritual things are very real, as real as the physical, and there is really no division between the physical and the spiritual."[30] It was within this system of beliefs, emphasizing the oneness of all things, that John brought together faith and art.

A final point that needs to be absolutely clear is that the arts are not a solution to the problem of declining membership in mainline Protestant

---

God. Their comments are generally absent in the reporting of this data, because while the arts continue to play a role in their *lives*, they do not play a role in their *faith lives*.

27. Mary, interview by Katherine M. Douglass, transcript, August 2011.

28. Erin, interview by Katherine M. Douglass, transcript, March 2011.

29. John, interview by Katherine M. Douglass, transcript, August 2011.

30. John, interview.

churches.[31] Neither are they an automatic fix to encourage vibrant faith in young adults or a sneaky way to lure young adults into congregations.[32] Rather, as we will see in what these young adults say, the arts offer a symbolic medium that often carries more clear or immediate forms of expression and communication of a message—sometimes opening them up to possibilities or relationships that they might not have otherwise pursued. The arts also function cathartically in congregations of the aptly labeled "frozen chosen," helping them make relational connections with their immediate community, rich history, and even God.[33] Through the arts, individuals have an opportunity to lead within their congregations in ways that affirm their God-given gifts and that extend beyond the scope of reading the lectionary passage for the week. In addition, the arts invite more meaningful and deeper levels of participation in worship and devotion practices.

These categories—expressing, connecting, and opening—have emerged from the voices of young adults as a result of the kind of listening that Wuthnow says we should do when we take talk seriously. It is impossible to deny the repeated phrases, patterns, and ways that young adults talk about the arts. They regularly use the terms "express," "expressing," "expression," and so on, when talking about their own participation in music, dance, or poetry. As we will see below, the themes of connecting, expressing, and opening often overlap. It is at these points, when a quote could easily fall into both the "expressing" and "connecting" categories, that the following sections seem to unnaturally divide the "talk" of young adults. I have done my best to highlight where these points are and to note that these may easily fit into another category.

---

31. One might be tempted to jump to this conclusion from reading Robert Wuthnow's book *All in Sync*, with the alluring subtitle, *How Music and Art Are Revitalizing American Religion*. While I believe that Wuthnow is correct in his assessment that the arts and music are playing a revitalizing role in American congregations, it would be going beyond the bounds of his claims to assume that more art equals higher congregational participation. In other words, he is claiming correlation, but not necessarily causation.

32. Richard Flory and Donald Miller have found that young adults have aesthetically rich and intentional faith practices; however, these are an expression of the faith commitments they hold—for example, those interested in monastic practices tend to light more candles and burn more incense. These aesthetic choices are dependent upon their faith commitments. Flory and Miller, *Finding Faith*.

33. This is a self-deprecating nickname those in the PC(USA) have adopted to highlight their style of worship, which rarely involves bodily movement.

Connecting

When young adults talked about the role that the arts played in their faith lives they often referred to "connecting" or used the word "connect." This connection was always between them and another. This "other" referred to those in the present, including their immediate neighbor, or those in a larger group, those from the historic past, and God.

Connecting to Others in Space and Time

Young adults spoke about connection with others both in terms of feeling connected relationally to those in the present, as well as actual physical connections. In order to interpret this finding it is helpful to return to Chaves, whose description of bridging and bonding is interpreted for the analysis of congregational life, especially with regard to the arts.

"Bonding" civic participation tends to keep individuals within the groups or associations to which they are primarily attached. "Bridging" civic participation, by contrast, connects people in one group or association with people in other locations. Some congregational activities are of the bonding sort; others create bridges to the world outside the congregation. This is as true for congregations' arts and cultural activities as it is for their activities in general. Some congregational arts activities directly connect congregations and their people to secular art worlds; others do not.[34]

The way that the young adults I spoke with talked about the arts was mainly in terms of bonding, that is, making or deepening connections within congregations. For example, Margot said,

> So I think that for some young adults it [the arts] can be the conduit through which . . . they get involved in church in a greater way, because I know sometimes in some churches, and it isn't the same in all churches, but there seems to be a gap between when you are in youth group and when you have kids, and you want to have a leadership role. As young adults, I feel like you can sometimes use involvement in church through art to be more involved in the church in a way that might not necessarily be otherwise.[35]

Margot indirectly named the programmatic abyss for young adults, identifying the "in-between" time when an individual is no longer in youth group

---

34. Chaves, *Congregations in America*, 170.

35. Margot, interview.

and when they do not yet have kids. According to her, the arts could be a way for young adults to have a place in the life of the congregation that they might not otherwise have.

A young African American woman, Karen, articulated a similar insight, claiming that many of the artistic talents that individuals have outside of church are a way for them to connect within church.[36] This seems to focus more on what Putnam would call bridging, although she mentioned the potential bonding qualities of this participation as well, which help youth to avoid feeling "lost."

> The role that the arts play for youth—young adults ages 18 to 30—that role is played in such a way that it engages their mind and their creativity to a certain extent. It is played out in various ways, as we were talking about, and I just think of the youth in my church currently and a lot of them are writers and dancers, singers and those types of things, and *they participate in those types of things even outside of church and in their schools.* They are in gospel choirs and gospel step teams and liturgical dancing and things like that. And I think it plays a role in the way that they function and they think about themselves within the church as a whole, and I think that *lots of times youth are lost in that conversation about their role in the church.* And, luckily, in our congregation anybody can be a leader if you are a member and have been baptized and [things of] that nature. So if you are 16 you can be on session, you can be a deacon, you can be a trustee. So incorporating the fresh minds of the youth in that worship service and bringing out their own ideas and creativity is something that is used in our congregation. And I think I may be going off the question a little bit. But I'm thinking that the role that it plays can be very major because that is how the youth function. They function in the age of text messaging and non-language words, and you say, "What are you saying to me right now, could you spell it out for me?" And this idea *of these communities where they are communicating all the time and they are brought into their spiritual world trying to connect them in a way that they can understand and broken down and made tangible for them.*[37]

For the youth and young adults Karen knew, the arts were an important part of their life both within the congregation, fostering bonding relationships, and outside of it, bridging various individuals through common aesthetic

---

36. Karen, interview by Katherine M. Douglass, transcript, May 2011.

37. Karen, interview.

interests. Karen concluded by saying that the goal of all participation of young adults, in their leadership as well as when they bring their artistic gifts into leadership roles in the church, is that they connect in a way that brings about mutual understanding. She assumed that the church has a responsibility to connect with young adults and make their message accessible. One way to do that is to learn what Karen called the "non-language words" of young adults so that real communication can take place. She included text messaging as well as the symbolic communication possible through the arts. Interestingly, both Margot and Karen said that young adults are "lost" or have no logical place in the church, but the arts are a mode by which it is possible for them to connect or, to use Putnam's term, bond.

Clay talked about how the arts provide a way for individuals to express who they are in order to be known: "I would again say that I think [participating in the arts] is a really good outlet or avenue for people to express themselves or deal with sometimes difficult issues in religion and life, and also a way for a person to show who they are and show off their distinct abilities that are their natural talent."[38] While Clay is directly talking about expression, it is clear that when we look at the content of what he says, part of the goal of expression is to share one's "distinct abilities" and "natural talent" so that others have access to seeing "who they are." This is especially important when considered in relationship to Margot and Karen's concern that young adults do not seem to have an obvious space to be seen and known in congregations.

When commenting on the bodily interactions of individuals during church, Mary shared these thoughts:

> On a day-to-day basis I think it is good that we stand up and sit down so we don't get sleepy, to differentiate parts of the service. And this isn't Presbyterian, they [at a PC(USA) church] all hold hands during the Lord's Prayer and I love that. I think that is so beautiful. So anytime there is hand-holding, great! Circles are very symbolic, so you can see everyone. I think there should be more touching. I like passing the peace and shaking hands, but I feel like each of us has such beautiful energy and our difference is what makes us so great and this is why we have different Bible study groups, so we can have different ideas together, but I feel if we even just touch to balance it out, it takes a lot of trust too. I love clapping and swaying.[39]

38. Clay, interview by Katherine M. Douglass, transcript, October 2011.

39. Mary, interview.

For this young woman, connecting with others involved literal touching, hand-holding, making circles, looking at each other, and experiencing the "beautiful energy" of each unique person gathered. As a dancer, she is likely more attuned to these bodily interactions than others. It is also somewhat countercultural for her to strongly embrace physical interactions when "political correctness" often stands in the way of these more intimate interactions. She also mentioned the diversity and difference among those gathered for worship and Bible study and highlighted this as "what makes us so great," and yet she commented that this is balanced out "if even we just touch."

Another young woman who is a student and participates in a dance team said that she feels "sync'd up" when she dances at church. "Sometimes I feel like in dance I can really sync up and that happens mainly at church," Erin said.[40] This particular woman talked about how she feels God's presence when she dances in both the congregational and performance context. When Putnam discusses bridging, he seems to mean the diplomatic function of a choir going out from a congregation to perform or a secular artist coming into a church to share their art. With Erin and others who were interviewed, this bridging seems to be much more individual and personal. The "syncing up" Erin felt bridges both worlds, bringing a common experience of connection with God to both. The arts not only bridge two worlds that individuals may otherwise believe are disconnected but also function as a bridge to connection with God.

Connecting to Those from the Past

When connection was mentioned, it was in reference to others both within the same vicinity or room (physically and relationally) and with those from the past. For example, singing a hymn connects young adults with a long tradition. Susan, who was quoted above, found older and international music to provide a more authentic religious experience. Another young woman, Kim, shared a similar sentiment:

> I love hymns . . . I really just like the old hymns a lot. The fact that they have been around for so long—that history tied to them. I am not really familiar with Taizé or chants, but the fact that these things have history tied to them, I think it makes them matter more to me. Because, *I feel like I am participating in something*

40. Erin, interview.

that . . . people before me that have participated in. I feel like a lot of these praise songs are a little too modern and you can't just develop that history and significance in that short amount of time.[41]

When asked what her favorite hymn was, she replied, "Holy, Holy, Holy."[42] Kim also said that she enjoys "singing hymns from all over the world, and [she] get[s] an idea of how other countries worship too."[43] Singing hymns aided Kim in connecting with a long history of faith, and also the global church. She assumed that the longevity of the hymns proved their significance. In other words, these songs have been meaningful to Christians throughout history, and when congregations sing them today they are participating in this continuing worship. She also mentioned Taizé and international music, not only for their enjoyable quality but also because they give her "an idea of how other countries worship." This quote shows the kind of openness that will be directly considered later.

Connecting to God

Young adults had a lot to say about connecting to God.[44] In answering the question, "Do you have any beliefs about God that inform the way you think about the arts or creativity?" Arthur said,

> Yes, I think that God is at once entirely accepting and loving and caring and literally this force of good and peace and tranquility. And so, a lot of times, you know, some artists that I enjoy more than others tend to be people—that is how they reach their calm state, or *how they get to God* is through the torment of their lives. They put it down somewhere. And in the act of putting it somewhere and putting it on paper they are able to reach that point

41. Kim, interview by Katherine M. Douglass, transcript, March 2011. Emphasis mine.

42. "Holy, Holy, Holy! Lord God Almighty," words by Reginald Heber (1826), music (NICEA) by John B. Dykes (1861).

43. Kim, interview.

44. Some young adults talked about the arts as functioning in a way similar to an icon, as a medium through which one connects with God. The scope of this research project does not permit me to explore this concept here; however, in future work I would like to consider the way in which the historic tradition of iconography may shed light upon this claim.

where God is there; *it's less that God is in their work, but that their work is getting them to God.*[45]

It is significant to note that this young man differentiates between God's presence in the work and the almost Reformed eucharistic description of the art "getting them to God." The art functions both as a repository for "the torment of their lives" and as a transporting medium that moves an individual into the presence of God. He claimed further that for him, it is not art in general that has this power to transport but specifically music. "Sometimes I feel like God is speaking to me through my iPod," he said. Elaborating on this same point, Margot said,

> The arts can really be this channel to connecting with God. Like a direct line that I don't get anywhere else in life, really, like reading the Bible, or listening to sermons or painting or visual arts or some things like that. It is really music that is the most intense and immediate way for me to be more present in God's Spirit.[46]

Arthur and Margot reflected that they are moved into God's presence through music and that God speaks through music. Others also interpreted their encounters with God as immanently present in the music they listen to.

Matt said that God has spoken to him through the song lyrics of Kelly Clarkson and Shania Twain—not so much in terms of these two women as individuals, but through the message in the words of the songs they sing. He explained,

> I was driving to work in the fall, and I was hating my life, and I was listening to Kelly Clarkson (as you do). I would say this is the first of a series of encounters with God—of God manifesting himself to me—and I didn't know what was happening to me in the moment. But, you know, I was listening to Kelly and zoned out and all of a sudden this one song came on and I wish I could remember the name of it, and it wasn't her singing anymore—it was totally God. You know, obviously, it still sounded like Kelly Clarkson and it was still Kelly Clarkson's song, but it was God, and there wasn't a doubt in my mind . . . It was illuminated in a completely different way.[47]

45. Arthur, interview by Katherine M. Douglass, transcript, August 2011. Emphasis mine.

46. Margot, interview.

47. Matt, interview by Katherine M. Douglass, transcript, March 2011.

He shared that he had a similar experience while running and listening to the Shania Twain song "You're Still the One." These experiences not only transformed the way Matt listened to the two songs, they were also personally transformative, as they connected him to God at a time when he was, as he said, "hating his life."

Emily also found that songs help her connect to an awareness of God when she is not in a worship service:

> I know sometimes I have certain hymns stuck in my head after church, and I think that can make one want to be more, get more involved with the singing or . . . [it] might make them want to explore painting or drawing that would help them during their devotional time, or something that would help them feel closer to God or something they could put up in their house and look at or, you know, kind of use as a religious symbol or something.[48]

According to Emily, songs or hymns that get stuck in your head or religious symbols placed in the home are both ways that might help individuals "feel close to God" or become more aware of God's presence.

Another young woman, Jackie, said, "God speaks to me through narratives."[49] When elaborating on this further she reflected on Jesus' ministry:

> I mean, God works in parables so much. God works in stories that might or might not have happened. We have a creation myth, and I think that says a lot about how God interacts with us. So if we are made in the image of God . . . our tendency is to tell stories . . . We are telling stories.[50]

Jackie's experience was resonant with Matt's. Both described encountering God as a result of God's choosing to use song lyrics or stories to speak to humanity. Jackie connected our human desire to tell stories to being created in the image of God. For her, the stories told in the Bible provide a model for how God might speak in more secular stories.

After our interview Jackie went on to write and direct a play, titled *Eden*, at her university, which I was able to attend at her invitation.[51] This play retold the story of the Fall in the form of midrash. Following the third

---

48. Emily, interview by Katherine M. Douglass, transcript, July 2011.

49. Jackie, interview by Katherine M. Douglass, transcript, March 2011.

50. Jackie, interview.

51. Swanson, *Eden*.

performance there was a "talk back" in which the facilitator asked if participating in this play had changed the way the six women who had acted in or
directed it thought about God.[52] One said her participation was an expression of her faith. For another, acting in this play provided an opportunity to
reflect on a familiar story in an unfamiliar way. When I asked Jackie about
this later, she said she was not sure if her play was a faithful retelling of the
second creation story in Genesis or not, but she felt that God was present
through the process of the creation and performance of the work. Through
her study of Scripture, writing, rehearsal, and directing—all for the purposes
of retelling a biblical story—Jackie felt connected to God.

Young adults frequently named God as the giver of artistic talent.
John bridged the notion of connecting with your unique creative gifts to
connecting with God. "There is always this expression or, like, this art or
creativity that is there if you take the time to connect with it, and capture
it, and share it with other people," he said. "So I think God is kind of at the
source of that, like, that creativity. *And so connecting with your creativity is
also connecting with God.*"[53]

Jenny articulated a similar sentiment, while also tying giftedness to
a responsibility to use one's gifts for the sake of the community. She said,

> I would say that the belief that I have is that God gives us all gifts.
> [*Pause*] Definitely, that ties in with music and faith and art. Because
> we have to use those talents that God gives us—not everybody has
> a musical talent, not everybody has an art talent, but those that do
> have that gift should use it in God's church and their own faith. I
> think that it is the whole thing that God is a generous and giving
> God and bestows stuff upon us that we must use.[54]

Jenny said that when an individual is given gifts, they are from God—but
they are for the community, as well as for the enrichment of one's own faith
life. According to Jenny, gifts expose our connection to God and demand
our connection with the congregation.

---

52. A "talk back" has become a common event following the performance of a new
play. "The process of developing a new play typically involves some form of public reading of early drafts. For the most part, this is useful; the experience helps the writer answer
questions about plot, character, theme, emotional involvement—all those elements that
we take for granted when we ask, 'Does the play work?' While sometimes these answers
come to writers during the performance, it's become standard procedure to host a public
discussion afterward and to let the audience express its opinions." Rush, "Talking Back."

53. John, interview. Emphasis mine.

54. Jenny, interview by Katherine M. Douglass, transcript, June 2011.

Erin saw a connection not only between God and the gifts given to individuals but also between God and the creation of specific pieces of art. When asked the question, "What role does participation in the arts play in the faith lives of young adults?" Erin answered,

> I guess expressional. God is in everything, and I almost feel like he almost has to be there because it is almost too beautiful not to have something behind it. And it could be something like ballet and I will still be crying at the end, like, this is so pretty to watch. And I feel like imagination and creativity are not something inherent in a person—I think it is a gift. I think certain paintings and certain sculptures are inspired or created through God. I feel like there are some very powerful pieces of art that there really couldn't be any other reason to explain it. To a degree. I know some people wouldn't agree with the pieces where I feel a connection to God, but I don't know.[55]

Erin saw God as facilitating and inspiring "certain paintings and certain sculptures." She acknowledged that everyone might not agree with her, but encountering these pieces makes her "feel a connection to God." Erin's statement could also fall into the "expression" category.

Leslie found theological truth in the medium of dance: "Yes, the action of it [dance] is such a present art form and somewhat worth saving, and I think God wants us to really not cling to the past too much or fret about the future, and you can dance in that way too."[56] The fleeting quality of dance gave Leslie insight into God's message of living in the present. Dance provided an analogy for understanding God's will.

Summary

In summary, young adults said that the arts help them feel connected to others in both bridging and bonding ways. Within congregations the arts can function to provide a logical place for the participation of young adults. The young adults in this study feel connected, or bonded, with others in the congregation when they use their artistic gifts, and in doing so they are known. These young adults sensed God's presence in both sacred and secular music, sculpture, paintings, and dance. In this way the arts were a medium through which God spoke or through which they

55. Erin, interview.
56. Leslie, interview by Katherine M. Douglass, transcript, April 2011.

were transported into God's presence. Young adults also participated in bridging experiences, like gospel choirs, dance groups, and theatrical productions in which their faith life was expressed outside of congregations, connecting them to others in their community.

Young adults said the arts fostered connection to others who were present but also claimed that singing hymns connected them with the past and, similarly, singing global or international music connected them with other cultures. These young adults claimed that the arts help them connect to God through the lyrics of music, as well as through the media of dance and storytelling. They also felt that the human proclivity for expression through an aesthetic activity such as storytelling was evidence of being created in the image of God. Finally, young adults saw a connection to God in the existence of their own unique giftedness and the aesthetic giftedness of others, which in turn fostered in them a desire to share those gifts with a community or name the presence of God when aesthetic beauty is expressed through the work of others.

Expressing

For young adults the arts also provide a means of expression. This expression took the form of singing, playing guitar, dancing, writing poetry, painting, journaling . . . and the list goes on. They described this expression as revealing their unique God-given identity and their true selves. This sort of personal expression sometimes was described as a confession of faith. This is especially significant for this group of young adults because of their affiliation with the Reformed tradition, through their involvement with a PC(USA) church or ministry.[57]

Expressing Identity

The arts function to help young adults express their unique identity—unique in the sense of being different from others and in the sense of being created in the image of God. It is clear from their comments that they have appropriated a sense of having been created by God and endowed by God with unique characteristics, gifts, and talents.

57. The significance of this affiliation will be elaborated on further in the fourth chapter, in which the tension between interpretations of the second commandment and congregational aesthetics will be considered.

Jason, who worked as a lay youth minister while in college before becoming a federal agent, described "recreation" as a time of "re-creation."[58] He said,

> I have a breakdown of recreation to re-creation and how God was our Creator, and we continue in that creation by our output. And I think it is paramount that—God gave us brains for us to use them, and one of the things we were given that no other critters were given was creativity and the ability to express ourselves. And so I think an expression like that is the only, really, the only natural response. That expression results in worship.[59]

Jason connected the uniquely human "ability to express ourselves" through creative acts with the act of worship. Similarly emphasizing the inherent value of aesthetic participation, Clay said that the arts provide both an "outlet" for expression of "natural" and "distinct" abilities as well as space for struggling with difficult issues. In his words, "I would say that I think it is a really good outlet or avenue for people to express themselves or deal with sometimes difficult issues in religion and life, and also a way for a person to show who they are and show off their distinct abilities that are their natural talent."[60] Mary similarly reflected that the arts provide an opportunity for the expression of individuality as well as love for God. She also commented on how the characteristics and medium of the aesthetic practices of young adults are different, making the expression of individuality unique for this generation:

> The arts help you express individuality and your love of God. This is possibly different than [for] previous generations. Our generation is unique. With where technology is and what we are able to do, and listen to, and be a part of, and I think, given—even our journaling has changed to online journaling, with blogs and sharing our art or ideas on the Internet. But that as young adults we honor God and include a wider variety of arts in our faith life . . . I think it is a really important part of where our generation is and what we are using to glorify God. And it is unique, and who knows what the next generation is going to get—they might express faith in a different way.[61]

58. Jason, interviewed by Katherine M. Douglass, transcript, October 2011.
59. Jason, interview.
60. Clay, interview.
61. Mary, interview.

Lisa also commented on the arts as especially important for "people [her] age":

> I don't know, after thinking about being creative and being part of God's creation, I guess I see the arts as a way for people my age to help figure out who they are as a person and who they are in Christ, because so much stuff in my life is indecision and, like, figuring out who you are and that kind of thing. And I think the arts—whatever you use to express yourself—can be a huge part of figuring out who you are, and I would like to think that if somebody was thinking about doubting in their faith or things like that, that it might be music or theater that brings them back, you know, that keeps them motivated and keeps them connected with God, that type of thing. And I think it can do that.[62]

For Lisa, the arts not only help express identity but also aid in the discovery of identity—not only identity generally, but identity as a Christian. As she said, the arts provide "a way for people my age to help figure out who they are as a person and who they are in Christ." Lisa additionally said that when people have doubts in their faith life—and perhaps we may assume she means they have become disconnected either from God or from congregational life—music or theater may be the medium that brings them back into a relationship with God and reanimates their faith. This claim echoes Wuthnow's finding in *All in Sync* that the arts can function as a bridge to a life of faith, just as a life of faith can function as a bridge to participation in the arts.[63]

Not only do young adults find the arts helpful as a tool through which they can express, wrestle with, or discover their identity, but they also see the expression of their unique artistic gifts as evidence of God's activity in their lives. As mentioned above, Erin answered the question, "Do you have any beliefs about God that inform the way you think about the arts?" in the following way: "I guess expressional. God is in everything and I almost feel like he almost has to be there because it is too beautiful not to have something behind it . . . I feel like imagination and creativity are not something inherent in a person—I think it is a gift."[64] Resonant with Erin's response, Arthur said,

---

62. Lisa, interviewed by Katherine M. Douglass, transcript, April 2011.

63. Wuthnow, *All in Sync*, 20.

64. Erin, interview.

I certainly think that every human has an artistic bone in their body, whether they believe it or not, just figuring out what it is and a way to express it . . . You start to exercise it, and it is hard not to see God in that every single time you do it, because it is something that was given to you and you have the ability to do that because you were born with it and it is in your nature. So I think that, in a sense, God is always informing what your ability is.[65]

Artistry or creativity (what Arthur calls "an artistic bone") is "given"—individuals are "born with it," and it is in each person's "nature." God is the source of this and continues to "inform" this ability, leading Arthur to claim that "it is hard not to see God every single time you do it." For Arthur and other young adults I interviewed, awareness and use of one's creative and artistic gifts is one way to know and reveal one's unique identity.

Weaving together the ideas of expressing identity and connecting with others, Mark said,

I believe that God created us with our different talents and our human bodies to use them. I don't know, *human expression and human creativity is part of what makes us human*—it is part of how *God created us to be creative and express ourselves* and things like that as a way *to connect with other people* and sometimes to work out our emotions . . . *He gave us music and arts and whatever other talents as a means of expressing yourself.* And that is what it means to be his creation is what we can be to be creative. And so that is an encouraging thing to me—that *God created us to be creative.* So, when I am trying out photography or journaling, and when I feel like I am just writing down word vomit or doodling, I feel like God created me to work those things out and that is what the arts would be for me. I have a good friend and his big thing is music and theater, and I can just tell, you know, with some people you can just tell that they were just created and they have those certain gifts. I don't know, it is just part of God's creation—is what I think is cool about that.[66]

Here he echoes what others have said about God having given humanity gifts with which to be creative, and this giftedness is an encouragement to him and an affirmation of his identity as a unique human. Mark also sees this in his friend, whose gifts are not photography or journaling but theater and music.

65. Arthur, interview.

66. Mark, interview by Katherine M. Douglass, transcript, September 2011. Emphasis mine.

He says that this "is just part of God's creation," which he thinks is "cool."[67] This proclivity to make and create art reveals a desire for connection and expression—to share or record symbolically something so that others, and even oneself, can return to it to recall an event or moment.

Along similar lines, of the unique gifts of humanity and human identity, Mark said,

> Well, it may not be 100 percent theologically sound, I think part of being a member of humanity, part of God's creation, is another sort of caveat. That being created in the image of God, it seems a lot of how to describe people are created. Because they have this seed in them, but I also think it can be tied to the arts in the sense that, you know, one of the persons of the Trinity is the creator God, Father God if you will, but creator God, and I believe that ability to create and make change lives within us—to a degree, of course. *Obviously I can't create matter, but I can create a song, and that song has real-world implications.* It may not have the same total impact as the female birthing the universe, but a song has the ability—music, arts, all these generally, even something as simple as a painting—*has the ability to change lives and make a real impact on somebody when everything comes together at the right moment.* A sermon, a song, what have you—it's when you are there and other people are there and the Holy Spirit is there, it all comes together and makes something.[68]

Mark drew attention to the analogous relationship of the human ability to create and God as Creator and one of the persons of the Trinity. He described a kind of creative synergistic collaboration between an individual, others, and the Holy Spirit. He saw the enactment of creativity in the world as being connected with the presence of the Holy Spirit. While he acknowledged that the creating humans do is different in kind from that of the Spirit, it is similar in that it has "real-world implications," with the "ability to change lives and make a real impact on somebody." The next chapter will reflect on the arts as a medium by which individuals express themselves and in so doing change the world, in dialogue with aesthetic

67. This is reminiscent of Wentzel van Huysteen's work *Alone in the World?*, which identifies the creation of art as one of the earliest activities of humanity, setting humans apart as expressing the *imago Dei*. This category will be expanded in the fourth chapter. Van Huyssteen, *Alone in the World?*.

68. Mark, interview. Emphasis mine.

learning theorist Maxine Greene.[69] Unlike Greene, a self-proclaimed atheist, Mark sees the Holy Spirit as active in the midst of these world-changing creative moments.

Jason, Clay, Mary, Erin, Arthur, Lisa, and Mark were not the only ones to comment on the expression of the *imago Dei* through human creativity. They represent others in this study and display the depth of theological thought in which these young adults are actively engaged. Leaders in the PC(USA) can celebrate the theological depth of thought and biblical literacy of these young adults. In addition, I believe their statements pose challenging questions to congregations. What opportunities do congregations provide for individuals to express their unique identity or the *imago Dei* within them? How do congregations participate in affirming the unique gifts of their members? And how do congregations respond when an individual risks this kind of expression?

Expressing Faith

Many young adults explained the function of art as a medium through which they express their faith. They commented both on their own practices as well as what they have observed in others. In many instances, their answers reveal the overlap of the categories of connecting, expressing, and opening. Susan answered the question, "What role do the arts play in the faith lives of young adults?" in this way:

> I think it can be an outlet and a way to express their faith; for some it is an act of worship, and for others it can be completely unrelated. I think music is a way to connect to other people, and in that regard, another way to connect with God. Art can cause religious experiences and art can be a religious experience, so it has serious potential to impact the religious life for people my age, but at the same time it may have none at all, depending on who it is.[70]

As Susan explained, the arts "*can* be an outlet and a way to express their faith," but this is not necessarily the case for everyone. She identified the connecting role that the arts can play relationally as well as serving as the catalyst for a religious experience. Like many others, Susan wanted to protect for those who do not find the arts to provide this kind of

69. Greene, *Variations on a Blue Guitar*; Greene, *The Dialectic of Freedom*; Greene, *Releasing the Imagination*.

70. Susan, interview.

connection or expression. Similar to Susan, Erin differentiated between the role the arts play in her life and the role that they play in the lives of others. While the arts, specifically dance, were important in Erin's life, she believed that the arts should be integrated without taking the foreground of her faith. She explained,

> [Art] is definitely not a primary role—it is not in the background, but it is not the first thing that comes to mind in terms of my faith. It is weird because I know people [for whom] it is the first thing—I have cousins that are in, like, gospel bands, and that is how they express themselves to God. But, at least for me, I think it is more "stand back," and it is more internal than like proclaiming my faith through the arts. And, basically, that is the way my church was at home. Well, actually, I think I might have been a little extreme with the arts and God. I feel like a lot of times people are going through the motions of it but aren't really making that connection. And then, for the churches in the South, I think it is all forced upon you rather than making a connection, so I really feel like it depends on the tradition that you grew up in. I feel like, with a lot of the students [in the college campus ministry in which I participate], I think it is more integrated but it is not in the foreground.[71]

Erin's hesitation regarding the use of the arts is resonant with the historic Protestant concern about the arts as a distraction from true worship, leading to idolatry. She said she was concerned that "people are going through the motions of it but aren't really making that connection" to God.[72] Erin went on to explain that she found the integration she experienced in the college ministry she was a part of to practice the kind of balance she was more comfortable with.

Regarding both the connection she feels to God through art and the role that the arts play in expressing faith, Jenny answered the question, "Do you have any beliefs about God that inform the way you think about the arts?" in this way:

> I would say that the belief I have is that God gives us all gifts. [Pause] Definitely, that ties in with music and faith and art. Because we have to use those talents that God gives us—not everybody has a musical talent, not everybody has an art talent, but those that do have the gift should use it in God's church and in their own faith. I

71. Erin, interview.
72. Erin, interview.

think it is the whole thing—that God is a generous and giving God and bestows stuff upon us that we must use.

In her interpretation, not only is God the source of each individual's unique gifts (a claim that is resonant with many of the young adults quoted above), but for those who have artistic gifts, there is an obligation to use them in the church and for their own faith. When placed in tension with Erin's statement, there seems to be a concern regarding the right or proper use of gifts. These concerns are resonant with the Apostle Paul, who in 1 Corinthians 12 names God as the giver of each unique gift and writes that those endowed with gifts have a responsibility to use them for the upbuilding of the community.

These concerns, along with Clay's articulation of how we are to use gifts in relationship to others, echo theological teachings on the right use of gifts, idolatry, communal life together, and care for neighbor. Clay's response to the same question broadens this concept. He shared his belief that when practiced, religion is "a lot about community and treating everyone like your brother and having everyone as your family."[73] For him this becomes embodied when he works in his part-time job as a disc jockey. He explained,

> DJ'ing is kind of like a family experience where you share the community of your brother and you are making them all and treating them all as you would want to be treated and enjoying each other's company, you know, and for me that is a direct expression, through my experiences, of the presence of God, I guess . . . Music in my life is directly related to that kind of love and passion that God has given us for our brother and family and community.[74]

For Clay, selecting and playing music is how he lives out his sense that God wants us to love our neighbor and consider each person to be a part of our family. Playing dance music for others gives Clay the opportunity to create a community where he senses God's presence—for him this experience is "a direct expression . . . of the presence of God."

Resonant with Lisa's earlier comments about the arts having the potential to bring an individual back to faith, Mark said,

> I think that along with life, I think it [participating in the arts] is one of the two things that can sustain young adults or anybody in their faith, in their faith journey and their life. But I think it has the ability

73. Clay, interview.

74. Clay, interview.

to heal wounds and to pick you up when you are feeling down, to add a contemplative feel to a situation, and to just keep you going—along with enriching [faith practices], of course, as I said the first time. An enriching experience, also sustaining us through harder times, at times when we are a little angry with God.[75]

For Mark, the arts enrich faith by "add[ing] a contemplative feel to a situation," "sustaining us through harder times," with the "ability to heal wounds" and "pick you up when you are feeling down."[76] Mark's comments name the ability of art to affect ambiance and emotion, as well as function to heal and sustain individuals during hard times. While he does not use the term "expression" or "express," it is clear that Mark believes that through participation in the arts, the faith lives of individuals are nourished, sustained, healed, and uplifted.

Summary

According to these responses, young adults seek out opportunities to express their identity and their faith through artistic activities that may evoke more emotion or create a more aesthetically vibrant ambiance. Many young adults believe that their unique gifts (artistic or otherwise) are gifts from God. They connect this belief with both greater knowledge of self and greater knowledge of God when these gifts are employed. This self-knowledge is linked to an awareness of their uniqueness, as well as insight into their identity as an individual and their identity as a Christian. Many used the language of being "created in the image of God" to describe this. Young adults believe God is present when they use their unique gifts and when they experience communal events where the arts play a central role (such as a group that is dancing together). Young adults are aware that the aesthetic practices they participate in, such as blogging, are likely unique to their generation. Finally, young adults seem to have an innate desire for connection to others through expression, or, as stated above, to share or symbolically record something so that others can return to it to recall an event or moment.

75. Mark, interview.
76. Mark, interview.

Opening

The final theme I heard among the young adults in this study was that of opening. The arts open them up in ways that increase their appreciation for the diversity and pluralism in the world and also open them up to the presence of God.

Those interviewed not only appreciated difference and pluralism but also sought out experiences, especially aesthetic experiences, that challenged them with alternative perspectives on how they interpret or perceive the world. This kind of pursuit of otherness goes beyond Putnam's "bridging" category because it involves more than building relationships with those outside of one's immediate community; it involves actively seeking out difference in order to see or think in new ways. They encountered ideological diversity within their families, peer groups, and worshipping community. Their appreciation was not limited to a relativistic view of plurality but included a deeper level of acknowledgment of human uniqueness and the freedom of God.

Open to Difference and Challenge

Young adults reflected both on the difference and challenge they find in messages that they encounter in secular spaces as well as within the Christian message. Reflecting on the sometimes ambiguous messages within plays or musicals, Elizabeth said, "It always comes back to what is the message, and how does it relate to what I believe, when I am preparing to perform or when I am seeing a performance."[77] I asked if she meant that she considered whether the message of the piece was resonant or dissonant with the Christian message. Finding value in art that is dissonant, she replied, "But if it is dissonant, does it make you think about what is right?"[78] This she found to be one of the values of theater, and she gave the example of a recent play she had seen in Chicago called *God of Carnage*, which is about two modern-day sets of parents and the disintegration of their friendship following a quarrel that their young sons had at school.[79] Elizabeth went on to say, "I think that this is what theater should be, more than just music and

---

77. Elizabeth, interview by Katherine M. Douglass, transcript, March 2011.

78. Elizabeth, interview.

79. *God of Carnage*, written by Yasmina Reza, directed by Rick Snyder, Goodman Theater, Chicago, Illinois, April 17, 2011.

performing, and it should make you think about what you saw instead of just being entertained for the whole two or three hours."[80]

One thoughtful young woman, Karen, suggested that I title my dissertation "Creative Christ" to highlight that God is the first one who is creative—who uses difference to attract the attention and following of millions of people. (This is interesting because it is not often the second person of the Trinity who is assigned the characteristic of "creative.") She explained how Jesus' gift of creativity was one of the main reasons he was able to attract individuals to himself, despite his radically different message.

> I think Christ himself was really creative. You have to be really creative to get someone to follow you. You have to do something, not just spectacular, but you have to dig deep to engage millions of people to even consider what you are saying to be a fact. It has to be at some different level, so that alone is creative. The creativity that he had to just go to other places that other people wouldn't even think of, like, was different, and creativity is something that is different and brings out something different than who you are as a person. And if you are one who will say, "I believe in Christ," then believe and reach for those people, believe and reach those who others don't want to reach—you have to be really creative to engage in that kind of way.[81]

Not only did she say that it is Christ who was creative in ministry, but she added that this translates into how people today must be creative in how they reach out to others—finding themselves to be different than they were before they knew Christ. Karen insightfully noted that creativity often means doing something challenging, such as reaching out to people whom others do not want to reach.

Within the Christian community Mary believed that God wants us to be creative in the diversity of ways we worship. She said,

> I mean, I think God wants us to worship Him in different ways, and I think there are a lot of different and valid ways in which to worship God through art. And maybe for me it is music, it is writing, it is drawing, but I think [that] for a lot of people, they can worship God and bring honor and glory to God through a lot of other mediums, especially through, like what I am thinking of is—I don't dance very well—but [a dance troupe on campus] would do some of the most gorgeous dances, and it was their way

80. Elizabeth, interview.

81. Karen, interview.

of honoring God. And I think God wants us to dance and sing and draw and use the talents that he gives us in whatever way works for you. The way you express it is like learning—if you were limited to one way, it wouldn't work. Different people do different things and feel closer to God in different ways, so I think God wants you to use whatever ways work for you.[82]

Similar to their statements on the contemporary versus traditional music debate, young adults were able to claim a preference while appreciating the different preferences of others. Mary was not flippant about this, but rather was deeply sincere in her acknowledgment that "different people do different things and feel closer to God in different ways."[83] She not only said that it was nice for individuals to be aware of different preferences but also claimed that "God wants you to use whatever ways work for you."[84] This is not a slippery slope into relativism regarding worship styles or devotional practices but actually resonates with stories from the Bible where individuals encounter God through a variety of ways, including a voice in a garden (Adam and Eve), a burning bush (Moses), a dance on the other side of the Red Sea (Miriam), a song sung after the conception of a child (Hannah and Mary), reading Scripture together (the Ethiopian eunuch and Jesus in the temple), lessons taught by a seaside (the Beatitudes and breakfast at the beach with the resurrected Christ), and a meal that proved more revelatory than a long walk and conversation (the two on the road to Emmaus who walked and ate with Jesus). In essence, Mary is acknowledging the personal relationship each individual has with God that is both unique and intimate and accounts for the unique gifts and desires of an individual. In many ways this theologically claims the freedom of God to accept human worship in whatever form is most sincere and true that comes from each individual. She is also claiming the freedom of God to reveal Godself to anyone in whatever form God chooses.

Along similar lines David responded to the question "What role do the arts play in the faith lives of young adults?" by saying,

I would define it individually because a lot of people, I mean, even when you are in a congregation, faith means something different to everyone in the room. I mean, my faith is different than how my mom views it, and my older brother views it and [my friend]

82. Mary, interview.
83. Mary, interview.
84. Mary, interview.

views it, and I'm sure it is slightly different than the way you view it as well. And that is what makes it so beautiful and interesting, and that is what makes art so interesting is that you have several different people with one religion viewing it differently. I mean, they still come from the same basis, but still there are things from within that religion that they view differently. You can get the same group of people and you can get them in front of a piece of art and have them see an *avant-garde* theater of the absurd and they will still find something else in it. And it is still that expression of that individuality that is pulled out from both of them.[85]

Similar to Mary, David found the different perspectives and interpretations of each person "beautiful and interesting" when they are considering both art and religion.[86] He added that humans are naturally inclined to make meaning from their experiences (i.e., they can see *avant-garde* theater productions on absurd topics and still make meaning from that experience). David saw this ability as something unique about each person as well as something they have in common. As we will hear from Maxine Greene in the next chapter, humans have an innate desire to interpret the world we encounter—and yet, as David said, our interpretations are unique.[87]

Open to God

In addition to the role that the arts play in helping them appreciate the differences among the individuals and communities they know, these young adults talked about how the arts and aesthetic encounters open them up to God and an increased awareness of God's presence. Kim shared the challenge of putting something as powerful as encountering God into words:

I mean, there is something there [in the arts]. I just can't verbalize it. It is sort of along the lines of why I love nature so much. It's like you can enjoy God's creation when you are out hiking around or walking around, and I feel you can do the same thing with music. But it is hard to express exactly why that is . . . If you let it take over you and you actually let it speak to you, like you do with

85. David, interview.

86. Ibid.

87. Hans-Georg Gadamer would attribute this to the unique historical trajectory of our lives, or our "historically affected consciousness." Gadamer, *Truth and Method*, 335–37, 350.

nature, then it's a very powerful feeling. And it could be a very spiritual experience.[88]

What I find significant in Kim's description is the sense of being "taken over" or giving oneself over to letting "it" (music, nature, or God) speak to you. This disposition is one where an individual must be open to the possibility of encountering God and receiving the message or experience that overtakes in holy surrender.[89]

In the following lengthy excerpt, Shannon shares how music at a concert, during a time when she served on a church committee, provided a definitive and surprising encounter with the Holy Spirit:

> Okay, I think, for me, [the arts are] one of the biggest parts of my spiritual life. I mean, in art as well as music, but especially music, it is something, for me, where I have felt the most spiritual reaction out of myself—with certain songs—and I especially like live experiences. Like at worship or at a concert, especially, [these] are really cool things. And, I think, that goes a lot of ways for other young adults for music, and especially for art when you are at a museum. But, I mean, art can be anywhere, and it can be a really interesting experience to witness that and feel tingly and . . . I don't know how to describe it, but that spiritual feeling. And the same goes for dancing and other art forms, but for me, especially, it is music [that] is a spiritual experience.
>
> I can get really specific. One of my favorite bands is Switchfoot—are you familiar? I have seen them live a couple times, and I don't know if this is getting really deep or something, but I didn't really know what the Holy Spirit was. Like, it has always been my "Father, Son and Holy Ghost," and I really started to get a better understanding for it while on the pastor nominating committee. And I think it was probably that same year that I saw for the first time Switchfoot live and the first time I ever felt like I was witnessing the Holy Spirit's presence. And so that was a really cool thing for me— and always a time that I have cited for myself as when I witnessed that. And I saw them again a couple years ago and it was the same thing—it is just such a cool, cool experience. And then Triennium, I went to—I went with [my friend] there, and especially the time we spent in worship there, especially the times we were all singing together—it is just so impacting, because it is, like, five thousand

---

88. Kim, interview.

89. I hope to pursue this playful disposition toward matters of faith in an article. Being consumed with playful encounter seems to have parallels with surrendering to God.

kids around your age, and adults, then all different people and it was just so cool. And especially that time when we were all singing together and, like, singing and dancing was just so awesome so, like, in worship and in those intimate times in different services here at camp [a local Presbyterian camp], retreats [and] stuff like that are really special experiences for me.

I don't even know how to describe it, because I guess it is a combination of everything: the energy in the building, all the people, definitely the lyrics. [In] 2006 or 7 was the first time I really felt the Holy Spirit for the first time; it was really weird.[90]

Shannon's explanation of her encounter with the Holy Spirit at a Switchfoot concert shows how music functioned to add the intimacy of a personal encounter to the intellectual knowledge she already had of the Trinity. The "really cool" experience of "witnessing the Holy Spirit's presence" happened the second time she saw Switchfoot as well as during a worship service at Triennium that involved singing and dancing.[91] Shannon's description of encountering the Holy Spirit as "really weird" exposes how this encounter was not necessarily what she had expected or experienced before. Despite this, her tone and enthusiasm suggest that she seeks out these "really special experiences" and goes into them with an openness to the possibility of seeing and feeling the Holy Spirit at work.

Jason discussed the disposition of being open to seeing the image of God exposed in the form of re-creation and creativity:

I think [the arts play] an important [role] whether [young adults] realize it or not . . . When I am looking at any kind of artwork, or thinking about all of the different kinds of music that I listen to, whether it is sacred music or not, I hear the re-creation in it. And whether the person, whatever their intent—whether they are Christian or not, faithful or not, in any sort of faith tradition—I really stand by the fact that God made us in his image and we are different and given brains and creativity, and I think it all flows from it.[92]

The kind of openness to God's presence in the aesthetic creations of others that Jason named has an eschatological quality to it. In music he hears "the re-creation" regardless of the intention of the artist. He is open to seeing the mysterious in-breaking of God's presence in the present, even in the diverse

90. Shannon, interview by Katherine M. Douglass, transcript, August 2011.

91. Triennium is an international gathering of PC(USA) youth that happens every third year and is hosted by Purdue University.

92. Jason, interview.

plurality of worldviews that makes up the artists of the world. Similar to Mary, what seems to be at stake theologically for Jason is the freedom of God in revelation. While others may not notice God's presence, Jason identified the creative work of individuals as an expression of being created in God's image—and this expression has re-creative and restorative power.

Summary

In summary, young adults are open to the different ways in which others express their faith while maintaining their own personal preferences. They are open to the idea that others encounter God differently and to the various interpretations others have of both art and religion. They are also not only open to but seek to name and protect for the freedom of God to speak to individuals in different ways. Aesthetic experiences open them up to encountering God as well as sometimes increasing their awareness of God's presence. They describe these occasions as happening at both predictable and surprising times. These aesthetic experiences that bring about greater awareness of God happen in natural settings—in the woods, for example, while on a hike—and "human-made" settings, such as a Switchfoot concert. Some, like Karen, were open to the way that Jesus' creative teaching might be a model for the challenging life that God calls individuals to lead. And some, like Jason, were open to seeing the future in-breaking of God's kingdom in the present through the beautiful re-creation made by humanity.

CONCLUSION

If we are to trust Christian Smith's analysis, the majority of youth and young adults are not very religious or theologically articulate, and they live out a faith that he calls "Moralistic Therapeutic Deism."[93] What I have found in the "talk" of these interviews contradicts some of Smith's conclusions. Of course, Smith does state that there are a few, the top 8 percent or so, who do have an articulate faith.[94] While it is possible that I stumbled upon thirty individuals within this top bracket to interview, it is highly unlikely, due to my sampling method. These were randomly selected mainline Protestants who collectively fall into the least theologically committed and articulate

93. Smith and Denton, *Soul Searching*.
94. Smith and Denton, *Soul Searching*, 220.

categories in Smith's studies. Instead, what has been heard through these interviews is that there are young adults who are very articulate about what they believe—especially regarding the presence and activity of God. These young adults have an articulate awareness and appreciation of pluralism (both within Christianity and religions generally). Through their reflections on their participation in the arts they expose a broadening landscape of faith practices. Obviously, my findings are different than Smith's because I asked different questions and used different research methods; however, given the nature of the question I was seeking to answer, I believe this qualitative approach of "taking talk seriously" through close readings of interviews ultimately proves more revelatory in its ability to describe the faith practices of young adults, even (and especially) when they do not conform to the standard measurements for religiosity (church attendance, Bible reading, and prayer).

For many, as we have heard, the arts aid in the expression of faith and identity, connection with others and God, and openness to diversity in the world and the presence of God. The arts not only bridge two worlds that individuals may otherwise believe are disconnected but also act as a bridge to connection with God. The arts also function to bond relationships within congregations—they draw young adults together and connect them to their denomination's history as well as to Christians around the globe. Awareness and use of their creative and artistic gifts is one way they discover and share their unique identity, both as an individual and as a Christian. In addition to the role that the arts play in helping them appreciate the differences among the individuals and communities they know, these young adults talked about how the arts and aesthetic encounters open them up to God and an increased awareness of God's presence.

In the following two chapters I will analyze the findings from the survey results and interviews through the lenses of aesthetic learning theory and Reformed theology. Whereas churches in the Reformed tradition have often been reticent to utilize the arts (often due to fears of idolatry), public schools have found the arts to have deeply beneficial qualities, not only in helping students learn in an enjoyable way but also in helping them consider the nuance and complexity of what it means to be a human being. In many ways the arts provide the field upon which the existential questions of life can be considered and reflected on in a public setting. In the next chapter I will argue, with John Dewey, that the arts are a mode of practical reason. Then I will use the work of aesthete and pedagogue Maxine Greene, who builds upon Dewey, as an analytical lens to further interpret and understand why many young adults find the arts to provide such powerful experiences of expression, connection, and opening.

3

RECOVERING THE AESTHETIC DIMENSION
OF PRACTICAL REASON[1]

INTRODUCTION

This chapter critically appropriates aesthetic learning theory as an interpretive lens to gain insight into the aesthetically rich faith practices of young adults. In summary, young adults participate in the arts to *express* their unique identity and faith, *connect* with others, their tradition, and God, and *open* up to diversity in the world and interpretations of God. I will use aesthetic learning theory to interpret these findings by making the following three arguments. First, there is an aesthetic dimension to practical reason, and without the acknowledgment of this dimension, epistemological claims about experience (including experiences of God) are incomplete. Second, participation in the arts provides the opportunity to ponder, express, and wrestle with deeply held beliefs about identity, as an individual and in relationship to others. Third, aesthetic participation is not merely formative and transformative in a secular sense, but forms and transforms the faith lives of young adults.

---

1. A similar form of this chapter was previously published in the journal *Religious Education* as Douglass, "Aesthetic Learning Theory and the Faith Formation of Young Adults."

The first section will use the work of American pragmatist John Dewey to argue for the unity of practical reason, and additionally, that the arts are a medium in which practical reason occurs.[2] Although the history is not recounted in this book, the term "practical reason" is being used because of its roots in aesthetic and embodied ways of knowing that connect thought and action. This lineage is traditionally traced through Immanuel Kant to Thomas Aquinas, and the emphasis has been on the relationship between thought (or reason) and action. In what follows, I will argue for a more integrated form of practical reason, a "unity" of practical reason, as claimed above, where thoughts and actions are not seen as separate, or hierarchical, but rather as various dimensions of the same event.

The second section will engage the work of aesthetic educational philosopher Maxine Greene, who continued Dewey's trajectory, to argue that the arts provide a medium wherein individuals encounter and interpret existential questions regarding identity and community. Finally, using Dewey and Greene as an interpretive lens, I will engage my qualitative research findings on young adults, the arts, and faith, to argue that as young adults participate in the arts they are not merely being formed or transformed in a secular sense, but specifically with regard to their Christian identity.

JOHN DEWEY: AESTHETIC EXPERIENCE AND PRACTICAL REASON

In *Art as Experience*, Dewey argued that aesthetic experience is not a separate epistemological category or mode of thought, but rather is one dimension of practical reason.[3] To argue this, Dewey provided a historical evaluation of the evolution of art as well as a philosophical critique of those whose ideas have intentionally or unintentionally separated the aesthetic dimension of experience from experience generally. According to

2. Dewey, *Art as Experience*.

3. Dewey uses the term "knowledge" or "philosophy"; however, I will use the term practical reason, because I believe this term highlights the complete epistemology that he is arguing for, which includes the embodied, aesthetic dimensions of knowledge. The term "practical reason" has been used by Thomas Aquinas as well as Immanuel Kant, and I will be using this in a different way—rather than thinking that leads to action, I want to emphasize the embodied (practical) dimensions of reason. While I do not engage their uses of this phrase in this book, I offer a critique of Kant's aesthetic philosophy later in this chapter. Aquinas, *Summa Theologia I-II*, 94, 2; Dewey, *Art as Experience*; Kant, *Critique of the Power of Judgment*.

Dewey, practical reason has historically been divided and teased apart into categories such as "reason and senses," or "theory and practice." Dewey's project was to clarify that, while it may be helpful to separate these categories for the sake of analysis, in experience, these divisions are not present, and when united constitute the fullness of practical reason or "knowledge." The significance of this claim is that a full epistemology (theological or otherwise) includes not only cognitive and discursive information but also the embodied, aesthetic dimensions of experience.

The Aesthetic Dimension of Practical Reason

Dewey identified a Platonic dualism in the history of what counts as practical reason. Priority had increasingly been given to abstract knowledge over physical, embodied experiences. He believed that art resists this division by affirming the philosophical encounter possible through encounter with or participation in art. In order to identify the lineage within which his argument falls, I will refer to the kind of knowledge he is arguing for as "practical reason."[4]

Dewey traced a distinct lineage exposing how art slowly became dissociated from daily life.[5] In the first chapter of *Art as Experience*, Dewey was concerned with biological human experience and the dimension of this experience that is aesthetic. *Art as Experience* begins by providing contemporary evidence of the division of art from daily experience. Dewey noticed that "when an art product once attains classic status, it somehow becomes isolated from the human conditions under which it was brought into being and from the human consequences it engenders in actual life-experience."[6] Instead, art is put on pedestals in museums to display the high culture of a country or to expose the breadth of its conquest (such as is on display at the Louvre, thanks to Napoleon). Rather than this modern conception of art, Dewey claimed that art and the aesthetic was

4. As will become clear below, practical reason, as opposed to reason alone, includes the embodied, practiced, and experiential dimensions of life in a definition of knowledge.

5. While I believe that Dewey's critique is absolutely correct for the Western world, I wonder if cultures that do not define themselves by conquest or have been victims rather than victors would be defined by the same artistic lineage. For example, in cultures lacking museums, are artistic artifacts and aesthetic experiences more common to daily life?

6. Dewey, *Art as Experience*, 1.

organic to daily life. Using the Parthenon as an example, Dewey asserted that in meeting the need for a place of worship, architecture and sculpture were born. Dance, song, and drama emerged from cultural and religious rituals. Pottery, woodcraft, metalworking, sewing, and weaving evolved to provide for the needs of daily life. Humanity has been and continues to be surrounded by aesthetically rich experiences. The divorce that has placed art in sterile museums, however, has trained humanity not to look for the aesthetic in the immediate.

Dewey longingly looked back to a period when craftsmen and craftswomen created beautiful objects that met the needs of the community. This example, among others, showed that the unity of practical reason was within society's collective memory.[7] In *Logic: The Theory of Inquiry*, Dewey discovered evidence of practical reason in Greek reflective thought.[8] He found that "in the early history of Greek reflective thought, art, or *techne*, and science were synonymous."[9] This unity broke apart quickly with Assyrian, Babylonian, and Egyptian influences that divided knowledge into "higher" and "lower" categories. This stratification took root in the Greek culture, eventually leading to divisions between philosophy and experiential knowledge. Philosophy was concerned with "rational" knowledge, whereas experiential knowledge dealt with "practical" issues. Dewey claimed that these divisions became manifest in the division between the philosophic leisure class and the more practical working class.[10] Thus the origin of the bifurcation "is itself socio-cultural."[11] This shift led to a generally accepted "contempt for the body, fear of the senses, and the opposition of flesh to spirit."[12] This resulted in a hierarchy, placing abstraction above physicality.

Dewey believed that the social implications of this epistemological division were problematic. "Prestige," he said, "goes to those who use their minds without participation of the body and who act vicariously through control of the bodies and labors of others."[13] The intellectuals, philosophers,

---

7. I believe that his description is a romantic oversimplification of the history of one trajectory of art that needs much more nuance. However, despite this flaw, his critique helps define an overarching problem with practical reason.

8. Dewey, *Later Works*, vol. 12, *Logic: The Theory of Inquiry*; Bourdieu, *Distinction*.

9. Dewey, *Later Works*, 12:77.

10. Dewey, *Later Works*, 12:79.

11. Dewey, *Later Works*, 12:79.

12. Dewey, *Art as Experience*, 21.

13. Dewey, *Art as Experience*.

and political leaders seem to have created, from the time of the Greeks through to the present, an elite class who value the "life of the mind" over life in a body. Dewey claimed that this unnatural bifurcation was not rooted in truth, but rather "in fear of what life may bring forth."[14] One result of this is that aesthetic experience has become intellectualized and considered contemplatively, in order to raise its status.[15]

Dewey believed this disposition toward art was wrong, because aesthetic experiences emerge from being and life, dependent on daily attentiveness to physical life. He further elaborated on the divorce of the theoretical from the practical aspects of art by stating that "the trouble with existing theories [about art] is that they start from a ready-made compartmentalization, or a conception of art that 'spiritualizes' it out of connection with the objects of concrete experience."[16] It is this critique of experience generally, and aesthetic experience specifically, that Dewey carries throughout *Art as Experience*, attempting to bring art down from the austere walls of museums in order to draw attention to the rational and sensuous dimensions of aesthetic experiences in daily life.

Aesthetic experience serves as a case study in practical reason. An aesthetic experience encompasses the subject and object, the intellectual and physical, the rational and sensual—all necessary and integral to the experience. Without both dimensions of these categories an experience would not exist. Therefore, Dewey critiqued the "professional thinker" as one who has been taught to divide these for analysis. He believed they were fooling themselves by believing that abstract thought is in some way higher or purer when the aesthetic dimensions of thought and life are removed.[17] As an example of this Dewey refers to I. A. Richards, who, when describing what happens when an individual encounters a painting, says it arouses a feeling of "beauty" within the individual rather than attributing any beautiful quality to the painting. The painting, for Richards, is a cause, and the effect on the viewer is a reaction of pleasure. This description makes it seem as though the "sensation" of beauty came from outside of the person,

14 I believe this inclination also comes from what Pierre Bourdieu would identify as the desire to distinguish oneself through one's taste for the abstract, for the purposes of social advance. Bourdieu, *Distinction*; Dewey, *Art as Experience*, 23.

15. Before Kant, this division, leading to a hierarchy of abstract, imaginative contemplation of the beautiful, was not as formally divided as it was after the Enlightenment. Kant, *Critique of the Power of Judgment*.

16. Dewey, *Art as Experience*, 10.

17. Dewey, *Art as Experience*, 261.

through the senses. Dewey uses the example of anger to refute this, saying that anger is not something that happens in us, but rather is at least partly created by us. Another example might be that two people, viewing the same painting, perceive it differently. What is different is not the painting but how they, as unique individuals with unique histories, perceive it. This example shows, as mentioned above, that we create aesthetic experiences and that our intellect and physicality are united—as we create anger in an experience we simultaneously feel angry, have angry thoughts and likely express our anger physically (even if this is merely through the tightening of our jaw muscles). In this regard, Dewey is in agreement with Kant, who affirms that imagination plays the role of a combinatory force that plays an active role, creating experience. Kant claims that this happens as the imagination brings together rational and sensuous experience. It is this assumed division, however, where Dewey disagrees.[18]

Dewey traced the trajectory of the unnatural separation of the senses and rationality through Immanuel Kant's *Critique of Judgment*.[19]

18. Dewey, *Art as Experience*, 261.

19. Kant's understanding of psychological theory was divided between our reason, which is our faculty of knowledge and understanding, and "sense-materials." Kant's major error, according to Dewey, was that he divorced thought from experience in this division. This divorce is made explicit in his *Critique of Judgment*, in which, Dewey says, Kant "bethought himself of a faculty of Judgment which is not reflective but intuitive and yet not concerned with objects of Pure Reason. This faculty is exercised in Contemplation, and the distinctively esthetic element is the pleasure which attends such Contemplation. Thus the psychological road was opened leading to the tower of 'Beauty' remote from all desire, action and stir of emotion."

In an effort to soften his critique Dewey suggested that Kant lived in a time of reason rather than a time of passion where representation was most valued in art. It is also clear from the passages referred to in *Logic: The Theory of Inquiry* that not only Kant but an entire lineage of thought is to blame in separating reason and the senses; however, Kant plays an especially foundational role in inciting this division.

Dewey went on in *Art as Experience* to elaborate the problems that arise from the initial division in Greek culture that were only made more distinct and given philosophical weight by Kant during the Enlightenment. The first problem is that these divisions lead to the belief that aesthetic experience is limited to pleasure. Instead, Dewey said that there is an aesthetic dimension to all experiences, including the non-pleasurable and grotesque. Second, Kant is unable to deal with bodies and the physicality of aesthetic experience. Dewey noted that for Kant "the uniqueness of the object perceived is an obstacle rather than an aid to the investigator." Against this, Dewey argued that the physical and sensuous dimension of experience is one aspect of the way that individuals "know." Third, these divisions fail to identify thought as integral to an aesthetic experience in the rhythm of expectancy and satisfaction. Kant would define an aesthetic experience as contemplation; however, this lacks the dynamism Dewey identified in experience.

Dewey summarized his main critique by proposing, "The psychological conceptions that are implied in 'rationalist' philosophies of art are all associated with a fixed separation of sense and reason. The work of art is so obviously sensuous and yet contains such wealth of meaning, that it is defined as a cancellation of the separation, and as an embodiment through sense of the logical structure of the universe."[20] Poetically he added, "Art is thus a way of having the substantial cake of reason while also enjoying the sensuous pleasure of eating it."[21] For Dewey, the aesthetic dimension of practical reason must be acknowledged. The logical corollary to this is that if an individual participates in the creation or perception of art, they are participating in practical reason.

Participation in Art as Practical Reason

Participating in practical reason is what Dewey claimed distinguished the artist from the craftsman. In aesthetic work, action and perception are both at work in giving meaning and form to something. The makers and creators of art simultaneously act, perceive, and evaluate while working on a project. This form of work integrates memories of past experiences, artistic skills, judgment, visionary ideas, and intellectual consideration regarding how these will come together in the creation of a new thing. Dewey claimed that in the creation of art the outward transformation of materials coincides with an inner transformation of the emotions and experience of an individual. Using the image of an exploding volcano, Dewey said that for the creation of art to be more than an outburst of emotion, time must elapse

---

Dewey said that if contemplation were redefined to include the physical dimension of an aesthetic experience that connotes a kind of dynamism within an aesthetic experience then he could agree. Curiously, to emphasize this dynamism Dewey uses religious imagery to express the active engagement of the whole person as one who desires, or has a disposition of expectation that is satisfied in an experience. He wrote, "In the kingdom of art as well as of righteousness it is those who hunger and thirst who enter." This dynamic interaction includes both physical activity and intellectual consideration. To explain this Dewey said, "Not only is art itself an operation of doing and making—a *poesis* expressed in the very word poetry—but esthetic perception demands, as we have seen, an organized body of activities, including motor elements for full perception." Dewey critiqued the "virtuous philosopher" who is stumped by the ability of the artist to dwell in the ambiguity of life and ability to consider the "dark side of things" while maintaining speculative distance. Dewey, *Art as Experience*, 263.

20. Dewey, *Art as Experience*, 269.

21. Dewey, *Art as Experience*.

for ideas and art to come to fruition out of the pressure forced upon it.[22] Art is seemingly spontaneous; however, this spontaneity is actually the culmination of a period of fermentation, or pressure building up to expression through a medium. Dewey used the metaphoric language of conceiving, pregnancy, and birth to highlight this process as one of fertile expectation as well as the independence of the created work in relation to the creator and perceiver once it is "born."[23]

In addition to the maker or creator of art, Dewey emphasized the important role of the perceiver in experiencing art. They too are a creator—however, they create an experience rather than a piece of art.

> A beholder must *create* his own experience. And his creation must include relations comparable to those which the original producer underwent. They are not the same in any literal sense. But with the perceiver, as with the artist, there must be an ordering of the elements of the whole that is in form, although not in details, the same as the process of organization the creator of the work consciously experienced. Without an act of *recreation* the object is not perceived as a work of art.[24]

This re-creation by the perceiver or beholder is significant because it means that a piece of art must be purposefully conceived and perceived as a work of art and this conceiving and perceiving must have continuity. It also emphasizes the active role of interpretation done by the perceiver, who creates an experience that in some way must harmonize or "include relations comparable" with the art created by the artist. To see joy and happiness in Picasso's *Guernica* would be to create an aesthetic experience that is at variance with the meaning intended by the artist. To relate *Guernica* to the 2012 conflict between the Syrian government and Syrian rebels would be to engage the surplus of meaning within the work, not initially intended by Picasso, but still able to speak into the present.[25] Both countries experienced the government attacking their own people. An individual must also be open to the message or meaning of the artwork—even when it may challenge the previously held beliefs or assumptions of that person. Dewey emphasized that "aesthetic" is not a quality inherent to an object, but rather it is our experience that experiences it as

22. Dewey, *Art as Experience*, 72.

23. Dewey, *Art as Experience*, 111.

24. Dewey, *Art as Experience*, 56. Emphasis mine.

25. Ricoeur, *Interpretation Theory*.

aesthetic. We create the experience as our past histories come into contact with this new thing.[26]

Dewey also drew attention to the notion of "expression," which signifies both action and result. Art is actualized intent—an expressing expression. Photography (as well as other media) has freed painting, for example, from simply attempting to perfectly represent something else, and now can solely exist to express the intent of its creator. Art does not replicate, but rather communicates. Because of its power to communicate, express, and provide a holding environment for reflective and reflexive thought, art and aesthetic experience redefine traditionally abstract notions of knowledge to encompass a richer, fuller quality. Especially with regard to art, but truly with all experiences—even experiences of knowing—there is an aesthetic dimension. Without attention to the aesthetic dimension of experience, Dewey argued, practical reason is always incomplete.

In light of this argument, Dewey asserted that art is the freest and most universal form of communication that exists. Indirectly, he meant this as a critique of exclusively language-centered education. "If all meanings could be adequately expressed by words," Dewey asserted, "the arts of music and painting would not exist. There are values and meanings that can be expressed only by immediately visible and audible qualities, and to ask what they mean in the sense of something that can be put into words is to deny their distinctive existence."[27] Pedagogically, this gives art a unique role in the education and formation of individuals that is unavailable through other mediums.[28] Art should not, therefore, be relegated as a lesser form of pedagogy, to be used only for the education and formation of children and the illiterate, but with all people.

Dewey's Responses to Various Critiques

To complete his defense of art as experience Dewey refuted some of the common definitions and critiques of art that divorce it from intellectual activity, especially in relationship to the imagination. Dewey lifted up

26. Hans-Georg Gadamer's notion of "historically effected consciousness" similarly emphasizes that our experiences are situated in a long line of experiences. Therefore, as we experience things our history affects the way we experience them. Gadamer, *Truth and Method*.

27. Dewey, *Art as Experience*, 77.

28. Dewey, *Art as Experience*, 282.

aesthetic experience as having an imaginative quality, a quality common to all conscious experience, and yet he pointed out that this was not the role for imagination that most aesthetic philosophers would affirm.[29] Dewey asserted that most philosophies of aesthetic experience tend to limit it to only one of its many qualities—such as sense, emotion, or reason—rather than embrace the multiple dimensions of experience. To those who said that the aesthetic experience is "make-believe," Dewey replied that while dreams, imaginative ideas, and "pretend" may inform an aesthetic experience, the experience itself is real and grows out of the real experience of the artist and the perceiver. In fact,

> while the roots of every experience are found in the interaction of a live creature with its environment, that experience becomes conscious, a matter of perception, only when meanings enter it that are derived from prior experiences. Imagination is the only gateway through which these meanings can find their way into a present interaction.[30]

Dewey agreed with those who said aesthetic experience is play, but only insofar as play is "work" that is not the random play of a kitten with a ball of yarn.[31] Art is play at work, as it has a purpose that is actualized. It transforms something from its natural state into something else.

To those who said that art was the "expression of a surplus of energy," Dewey replied that assumed in this statement was that freedom is attained only by means of escape.[32] Art, however, is not escape but purposeful engagement manifest in expression. To those who said artists were merely expressing individuality, Dewey replied that while they are unique individuals, artists are situated, and their art is recognizable and received by others and therefore is not so "individual" that they are unable to connect with others.

To those, such as Plato, who said that art was a means by which to climb a ladder of understanding toward truth and essence, Dewey replied that reason is transformed by knowledge that is "effected in imaginative and emotional vision, and in expression through union with sense-material

29. Dewey, *Art as Experience*, 283.

30. Dewey, *Art as Experience*.

31. Dewey, *Art as Experience*, 290. In his *Democracy and Education*, Dewey argued for the pedagogical value of play and noted that art, for adults, is the main form of play. Dewey, *Democracy and Education*, 206.

32. Dewey, *Art as Experience*, 291.

and knowledge."[33] However, this transformation of reason is not because the art is a channel to the divine but because art communicates universals that convict and awaken our past experiences.

Dewey spent considerable ink clarifying his definition of imagination, perhaps in order to separate it from Kant's. Despite his attempt to differentiate himself, he found value in Kant's categories, as is evident when he said, "There is always some measure of adventure in the meeting of the mind and the universe, and this adventure is, in its measure, imagination."[34] Consequently, he claimed that "possibilities are embodied in works of arts that are not elsewhere actualized; this *embodiment* is the best evidence that can be found of the true nature of imagination."[35] According to Dewey, imagination is not, as Kant claimed, the combinatory force that internally contemplates between reason and sense-materials, but instead actively takes form externally, such as in a work of art, where the individual interacts with the world.[36]

At this point we might ask, Why art? Why has art been used as a case study or as proof of the unity of rationality and sensuality in practical reason? Dewey explained that it is what philosophy and art have in common that ultimately proves his point. In fact, no other medium can provide a better embodiment of philosophic thought, or practical reason. For philosophy, like art, moves in the medium of imaginative mind, and since art is the most direct and complete manifestation there is of experience *as* experience, it provides a unique control for the imaginative ventures of philosophy.

> In art as an experience, actuality and possibility or ideality, the new and the old, objective material and personal response, the individual and the universal, surface and depth, sense and meaning, are integrated in an experience in which they are all transfigured from the significance that belongs to them when isolated in reflection . . . Of art as experience it is also true that nature has neither subjective nor objective being; is neither individual nor universal, sensuous nor rational. The significance of art as experience is, therefore, incomparable for the adventure of philosophic thought.[37]

---

33. Dewey, *Art as Experience*, 303.
34. Dewey, *Art as Experience*, 278.
35. Dewey, *Art as Experience*, 279.
36. Dewey, *Art as Experience*, 280.
37. Dewey, *Art as Experience*, 309.

Art as experience embodies what Dewey believed to be philosophical thought—embodied, dynamically engaged, historically effected, and situated.[38]

One additional note: Dewey curiously compared innovative artists to the biblical prophets who were stoned for the ingenuity and challenge to their communities. He compared them on the basis of what is at stake for both: revelation. "'Revelation' in art," he said, "is the quickened expansion of experience. Philosophy is said to begin in wonder and end in understanding. Art departs from what has been understood and ends in wonder. In this end, the human contribution in art is also the quickened work of nature in man."[39] Power, influence, truth, and understanding are at stake in art as experience. It is natural for humanity to inquire and interpret. At its core, art as practical reason, like philosophic thought, does this work. Like practical reason, art makes warranted assertions about reality, but despite its urgency does not make ultimate truth claims.

MAXINE GREENE: AESTHETIC EDUCATION AND TRANSFORMATION

In order to appropriate John Dewey's theories for the present we will engage the work of aesthetic educational philosopher Maxine Greene. Greene's writings and speeches are not systematic, but rather circle around themes. These themes include the construction (or creation) and transformation (or re-creation) of identity, the pursuit of freedom within a democratic society, and the value of pluralism, difference, and otherness. These themes build

38 In an attempt to expose just how severe this idea, is Richard Rorty states, "Dewey wants the distinctions between art, science, and philosophy to be rubbed out, and replaced with the vague and uncontroversial notion of intelligence trying to solve problems and provide meaning." While I am not completely convinced that Dewey wants the distinctions totally rubbed out, I believe that Rorty is right to point out that for Dewey both art and philosophy are about the same work, which is to "solve problems and provide meaning." Rorty, "Overcoming the Tradition," 301.

39. Dewey, *Art as Experience*, 281. This quote resonates with John Calvin's opening words in the *Institutes*: "No one can look upon himself without immediately turning his thoughts to the contemplation of God, in whom he 'lives and moves' [Acts 17:28]." In this passage, without giving attention to it, Calvin shows a bodily connection with knowledge of God. This expands in later chapters as Calvin interprets passages such as Psalm 19 as declaring the knowledge of God found in creation. Calvin, *Institutes of the Christian Religion*, I.1.1.

from Dewey and actualize them for the formation and transformation of individuals—and ultimately society.

The Transformative Power of Art

One danger Greene saw in our highly success-driven culture is that "young people find themselves described as 'human resources' rather than as persons who are centers of choice and evaluation."[40] When they participate in the arts, however, young people are "made aware of [themselves] as questioners, as meaning makers, as persons engaged in constructing and reconstructing realities with those around [them]."[41] Greene claimed that the purpose of aesthetic encounter is not to become a great artist, or even to like or appreciate art, but to be transformed. Transformation, according to Greene, is one of the *teloi* of aesthetic participation:

> The end in view . . . is *not* the ability to replicate, to recite, to demonstrate the mastery of skills. What we are trying to bring about is neither measurable nor predictable. How could it be if our desire is to enable persons to be personally present to works of art? How could it be if we want so deeply to enable persons to reach out, each one in his/her freedom, to release his/her imagination, to transmute, to transform?[42]

This theme—the transformative power of art—resounds repeatedly in *Variations on a Blue Guitar,* a collection of lectures she gave during teacher training sessions at the Lincoln Center in New York City. Art does not exist to be conquered or ingested, nor should knowledge about art differentiate an individual as elite.[43] Instead, Greene argued that art is something to be

40. Greene, *Releasing the Imagination,* 124. This lack of meaningfulness in daily work was highlighted by Levine and Heimerl in *Handmade Nation,* a study of the contemporary craft movement. Some crafters said that their crafting is a form of self-expression and creativity that adds to their life in a way that their daily work does not.

41. Greene, *Releasing the Imagination,* 131–32.

42. Greene, *Variations on a Blue Guitar,* 30.

43. This topic of aesthetic participation as an act of distinguishing oneself is worthy of its own research project. From my own research findings I do not believe that these young adults are participating in the arts in order to distinguish themselves. Many do, however, come from wealthier, highly educated families, and as a result they were able to participate in music and dance lessons as children. The PC(USA) is known for being one of the wealthier, more educated denominations and so there is likely a correlation here. In an attempt to make the arts accessible to all, Greene created a foundation that

engaged, and through that engagement it can open up an individual to being transformed. In this vein, she admonished educators to get beyond "art appreciation" and "art history" to actually engaging art so that people are "opened up" and "transformed."[44]

Resonant with Dewey, Greene said that as individuals make and create they are interpreting and making meaning of their experience—they are participating in practical reason. She additionally claimed that individuals are never merely creating but also re-creating—and what is being created and re-created is not merely art but individuals and the world. For Greene, what is at stake in this claim is that participation in art does not simply form individuals, telling them "you are this or that," but it transforms them, playfully opening up a myriad of possibilities for identity and relationships. She writes,

> First, I would affirm the value of making, shaping, expressing—of releasing as many persons as we can into the adventure and discipline of working with the materials of paint, sound, language, body movement, clay, voice, and film. There is no human being, no matter what age, who cannot be energized and enlarged when provided opportunities to sing, to say, to inscribe, to render, to show—to bring, through his or her devising, something new into the world. But there is more. It is largely through some immediate involvement with "making" (or, if you like, creating) that individuals who are not themselves artists can begin to get a sense of what is demanded by what might be called artistry. To understand on any level what excellence implies in this domain is to be acquainted with more than visible or audible products and achievements. It is to know something of the process, the craft. *It is to become in some way acquainted with the long trying, the self-reflecting, the rehearsing, the remaking, even the doubting* . . . If we can provide occasions for more and more to incarnate this somehow, make it integral to what they do day to day, then we will be able to tell ourselves that we are authentically in search of excellence—excellence as a way of conducting one's life, one's very being in the world.[45]

The process of making concerns reflection on existence. As she argued, the making and creating of art is beneficial not only for artists but for everyone.

---

supported art experiences for low-income communities. A history of the foundation and its projects can be found at the following web address. http://www.maxinegreene.org/. Accessed August 22, 2012.

44. Greene, *Variations on a Blue Guitar*.

45. Greene, *Variations on a Blue Guitar*, 202. Emphasis added.

Participation in the arts provokes one to ask, "*Who* am I, and what is the most excellent and true version of myself?" not merely "*What* am I?" with regard to profession or an identity imposed by others. Greene critiqued the media as expertly giving the accepted definition of reality. She challenged this by encouraging individuals not to "*accede* to the world as 'given'" but to imagine alternative realities, thus encouraging individuals to transform both themselves and the world.[46] According to Greene, the arts provide a medium for this kind of reimagining and remaking.

When the arts are engaged, the goal is not mastery or replication, as noted above, but rather wondering, in the mode of practical reason, through imaginative and playful encounter, with the potential result of transformation. Indeed, Greene pointed out that there is a limited human capacity for predicting and measuring the outcome of aesthetic encounters. Even so, the arts are a tool that facilitates the imagination in reimagining the world, and oneself, as otherwise.

Transformation toward Freedom

Greene claimed that the ultimate *telos* of aesthetic encounter, as engaged through pedagogical practices, is freedom. All transformation is toward greater freedom. Her understanding of freedom grew out of her background in John Dewey, Paulo Freire, and feminist theory and is therefore a democratic, liberative, and communal understanding of freedom. In *Dialectic of Freedom*, she claimed that the arts create space where awakening can occur and where individuals can encounter positive freedom.[47] This positive freedom is active and involves individuals becoming increasingly self-aware and making positive efforts to change themselves and the world. She said people must name and see the obstacles by becoming aware of them and then act in resistance to make space or "an opening" in the public sphere.[48] This space and "opening" happen naturally as individuals participate in the arts.

46. Greene, *Variations on a Blue Guitar*, 30.

47. Greene, *The Dialectic of Freedom*.

48. This claim is resonant with Paulo Freire's concept of *conscientization*; however, Greene chooses not to use this term. While she does not explain why, I believe it may be in order to emphasize the transformation of not only social and political location but also self-perception and identity.

Greene critiqued the American libertarian definition of freedom, which she interpreted as an individualistic, negative freedom—freedom from having your life affected by others. Instead, she defended communism's claim that true freedom acknowledges the interconnections between the well-being of all individuals.

A THEOLOGICAL ASSESSMENT OF DEWEY AND GREENE

In order to engage Dewey and Greene on the topic of Christian education and formation, it is necessary to consider the theological claims that are present either explicitly or implicitly in their work. Neither Greene nor Dewey made explicit religious claims in the works referred to here. Even so, it is interesting to note the theologically heavy terminology employed by both.

Dewey

As noted above, Dewey used the concept of revelation to describe progress in art. Revelation, according to Dewey, is the "pressing forward" of humanity embodied in works of art; however, this anthropocentric revelation is not the revelation of God. Even so, Dewey complimented the church for its attentiveness to the aesthetic dimension of experience through smells, bells, decoration, song, and drama.[49] Despite this compliment, Dewey's insight about the neglected aesthetic dimension of practical reason sheds a challenging light on the linguistically oriented educational and formational practices within the Reformed tradition. In addition to his claims about aesthetic experience, Dewey claimed that the arts unite humanity both in the present and within their evolutionary history. "Art," he said, "is the extension of the power of rites and ceremonies to unite men, through a shared celebration, to all incidents and scenes of life . . . That art weds man and nature is a familiar fact. Art also renders men aware of their union with one another in origin and destiny."[50]

It is clear from this quote that Dewey believed that as we look to art, humanity's creation, we cannot help being made aware of the interconnectedness

49. Dewey, *Art as Experience*, 31.

50. Dewey, *Art as Experience*, 282.

of humanity. This anthropocentric strain in Dewey leaves no room for an awe of creation that leads to an awe of the divine. Additionally, he does not identify this desire to connect as potentially a God-given desire. Despite these critiques, I do agree with Dewey that through art, humanity is able both to express and be united around their meaningful interpretations of the world. I would simply add that these relationships include the divine and the mark of the divine, or the image of God, within humanity.

Dewey's critique of practical reason as being unnaturally bifurcated into abstract and embodied dimensions sheds light on the historical struggle of the Reformed tradition to deal with the arts in light of the second commandment. The arts embraced by the Reformed tradition, specifically the PC(USA), have been those that are the most abstract—music and the spoken word (i.e., preaching)—because they seem the least prone to lead individuals into idolatry. This choice, as well as the use of visual arts with children and the illiterate, has resulted in a hierarchical structure of Christian formation within churches that identifies the arts as something to be employed within the faith of children in a way that prepares them for the more advanced experiences of worship, which demands much from the ear but little from the eye, nose, mouth, or body.

Theologically, this is significant—it names the division between the "incarnate" and "transcendent" as problematic. Using Dewey's rationale we might claim that these categories are helpful for the sake of analysis but become problematic when one dimension is emphasized over the other. It is theologically problematic to emphasize the resurrected Jesus apart from his bodily life and crucifixion. In educational practices, to teach about God the Creator without regard to the creation (and vice versa) is problematic. To discuss God the Holy Spirit without reference to the indwelling of the Spirit with and through God's people throughout time is problematic. This list could go on. Dewey's critique is helpful, because it challenges unnatural and unnecessary divisions within the realm of practical reason as well as practices of Christian education and formation. This is especially enlightening when we consider the fact that the arts facilitate young adults' knowing and being known by God and others. Their knowledge is embodied and abstract, including feelings, emotions, senses, imagination, and rationality. In many ways, their claims challenge the Reformed tradition to affirm their aesthetic experiences of God as both real and legitimate—and even, perhaps, as something to be more faithfully integrated into the life of the church.

Dewey is helpful because he explained that artistic participation embodies philosophical reflection, while acknowledging the aesthetic dimension of all experience. With regard to this project this is helpful for two reasons. First, it is clear that young adults are doing not only philosophical but also theological reflection as they make or encounter art. They believe that as they express, connect, and open up through participation in the arts, their knowledge about themselves, others, and God is changed, opened, and transformed. When they attend concerts, dance, hold hands, DJ, play guitar, sing, and read fantasy literature, they are reflecting upon theological and existential issues in a way that is transformative. Second, Dewey's insights about the often neglected aesthetic dimension of practical reason sheds a challenging light on the formational practices within the Reformed tradition, which tend to favor the mind. Could it be that these young adults are participating in the arts out of a sense of "a starved imagination," as Robertson Davies' character Arthur states in the epigram of this book? Is their artistic participation potentially exposing a yearning for a more embodied life of faith?

Greene

Greene's translation of Dewey's philosophical work into aesthetically rich pedagogical practices is helpful for interpreting this research. Her concepts of imagining the world as otherwise, opening space, and pursuing freedom name the unique value that the arts can potentially play when engaged beyond the mode of art history or art appreciation. Instead, she proposes that in order to embrace the full potential of the arts to engage in practical reason we must involve people in the making and creating process. When viewed through this lens, it becomes apparent that in many ways Greene explained what many young adults are doing—participating in the arts in order to *open* space for others, *express* (in freedom) what they believe or are wrestling with in terms of their identity, and *connect* with others empathically. While Greene and Dewey both draw our attention to a missing piece of practical reason—the aesthetic dimension—both have overlooked the spiritual dimension.

Greene was an atheist and so her use of the term "transformation," specifically toward freedom, finds its *telos* in American democracy interpreted through a feminist lens. She regularly used terms like "incarnate," "awakening," "creation," and "re-creation" without commenting on their theological weight. Her reader is left with the nagging question, To what end? That is, transformation from what to what? Awakening to what? Re-creation toward or into what? The notion of being gifted by God or transformed into the likeness of something (or someone) else does not exist for Greene. While Greene moves our thinking regarding pedagogical practices into significantly deeper reflection, it comes to an abrupt halt with any questions about the source of human uniqueness, or with whom we are seeking to connect beyond the human realm.

In theory, I agree with Greene. I believe that it is good—even ideal—when individuals grow in their self-awareness, confidence, and security in their identity, as well as their love of others and otherness. Personal growth, when the spiritual dimension is accounted for, includes deeper truths than secular philosophy has to offer. Reconciliation in the form of learning to love those we hate, forgiveness of those who are unrepentant, and the belief that life can come from death—these transformations are connected with our conformity to the likeness of Jesus Christ and living into the truth that each individual bears the image of God. This kind of spiritual or religious self-awareness is missing from Greene and Dewey.

There is a normative claim missing in Greene's work concerning the true identity of individuals. For Christians, identity is always formed and transformed in relation to someone—Jesus Christ. Christian love includes the radical imperative to love your enemies and those who persecute you. The freedom Christians pursue includes the choice to obey, to carry one another's burdens, and to claim responsibility for the well-being of the neighbor. Finally, the openness to possibility and mystery that Greene encourages is limited when the miraculous and surprising leading of the Holy Spirit is ignored. Within Greene's schema, religion and faith traditions restrict rather than transform—only art is given this power.

CONNECTING, EXPRESSING, AND OPENING VIEWED THROUGH THE LENS OF AESTHETIC LEARNING THEORY

When the aesthetic educational philosophies of Dewey and Greene are placed in conversation with the results of this study, it becomes clear that young adults are interested not merely in abstract forms of knowledge of God but in embodied, physical forms of connection that highlight the immanent, communal, and incarnate dimension of the Christian life. Rather than succumbing to being cast as "human resources," the young adults I interviewed are participating in the arts to express their identity and faith, to connect with others and God, and to be opened to new and different ways of worshipping and encountering God and otherness. When they participated in the arts they were not merely acquiring art skills or art appreciation—in fact, that was nowhere present in any of the interview results. Instead, through their participation in the arts, they claimed to become more aware of their unique Christian identity.

Expressing

Both Dewey and Greene comment on the power of art to facilitate the expression of the artist. Dewey's metaphors of the exploding volcano and pregnancy emphasized the need for expression that follows active and fertile periods of life. This explanation of the urge and need to express is helpful in understanding why young adults sought out opportunities to have aesthetic experiences, whether individually or communally. The making process invites the creative stirring and fermentation wherein individuals wrestle with what they believe to be true about their identity as well as their relationships to others, the world, and God. This internal wrestling seeks an outlet for expression, and for some this happens through art.

When they participated in the arts as a means of expression, many young adults felt that they were known. They said that they felt affirmed in their use of their own gifts and believed that others knew them more intimately when they shared their artistic gifts. Many found that the arts allowed them to share their God-given artistic gifts publicly, in a way that others could encounter and respond to. This experience was positive for them in that it affirmed their giftedness and identity, and it also affirmed their self-understanding when others perceived them in a way that was resonant with their impressions of themselves. By participating in art as a means of expression, young adults came to a fuller knowledge of themselves as unique and gifted by God. In using these gifts, they also claimed that their expression through art was an act of love for God.

Dewey would claim that these young adults engaged in practical reason as they used art as a means of expression. This practical reason included both aesthetic and spiritual dimensions. Whether in private or public, young adults felt that participation in the arts facilitated and embodied theological reflection as they engaged the arts as a form of expression.

Connecting

During the interviews I asked individuals to tell me about a time when they experienced God's presence. While many had fully developed understandings of God, none of them replied that they experienced God all the time, but instead described a moment or an event—a concert, for example, or a hike. Their descriptions were not abstract; they described song lyrics, writing in a journal, or feeling at one with others who were dancing and singing. These experiences certainly had abstract qualities, but they were also embodied and physical. The moments of connection with God happened in physical places with sounds, sights, and smells. These "connecting" encounters with God are resonant with Dewey's claims about the multifaceted dimensions of practical reason. Their knowledge of God and their awareness of God's presence happened during their daily life.

The young adults I interviewed described the arts as helping them connect in congregations that do not always have an obvious place for them. The arts also connected young adults with their own historical faith tradition. While Greene did not comment on the appreciation of tradition, she would affirm the ability of the arts to help individuals imaginatively connect with the experience of others as they "perceive alternative realities." Young adults claimed that singing hymns and songs from Taizé made them feel connected with their traditions and with others around the world. Dewey helps to explain this phenomenon in his claim that when encountering art, both the maker and the perceiver create an experience. Greene added the affirmation that encountering difference and otherness helps individuals to reflect on reality anew, challenging them to understand others in a deeper way that affirms the freedom of each.

Opening

In my research, I found that young adults were not merely open to having aesthetic encounters that were foreign to them but often sought them out. They were also open to different or unfamiliar conceptions, images, or interpretations of God. These different interpretations sometimes transformed their own understanding of God—broadening, deepening, or strengthening it. The goal of the young adults I interviewed was never replication or mastery as they participated in art (just as those are not the goals of a life of faith), but rather attentive encounter around the existential topics of identity, community, and otherness—and God, or life with God. Additionally, they claimed that God was free to use a variety of means of revelation for different people.

While some were likely very good guitar players, painters, dancers, or DJs, they did not identify excellence or professionalism as the reason they participated in an art form (although I do know that one has become a professional playwright). Instead, young adults discussed the value of participation. The value was in the doing and making and the community that involved, as well as the connection they felt with God as they used their God-given artistic gifts. This claim is resonant with Greene's claim quoted above that for all of humanity there is value in "making, shaping, expressing."

CONCLUSION

This chapter used the work of Dewey and Greene as an analytical lens through which to view the claims of young adults with regard to their participation in the arts. The arts function as practical reason in the faith lives of young adults, and through their participation both they and the world are transformed. As young adults create or encounter art they are making existential and theological claims such as these: "In this song you will hear who I am"; "When I read this novel it shifts my beliefs about God"; "When I see you dance I understand the way we are connected differently"; "The image of God you hold dear challenges what I previously believed about God"; "When we sing this song I feel connected to others, both globally and in the past." In these claims (which are interpretations of themselves, the world, and God) they and the world are transformed. What is at stake for the church, specifically with regard to practices of Christian formation, is whether the claims of these young adults are embraced as transformative for these individuals and their communities or, instead, are treated as interesting hobbies or, dare I suggest, problematic. In the following chapter, these findings will be raised to challenge the Reformed tradition, which has historically claimed that the arts are helpful as an aid to those with an immature, less abstract faith. Informed by the doctrine of the *imago Dei* as interpreted by Wolfhart Pannenberg and Wentzel van Huyssteen, I will argue that the process of creating and making is uniquely human and something that should be embraced through all of our living years.

4

THE IMAGE OF GOD, ART,
AND CHRISTIAN FORMATION

INTRODUCTION

In this chapter I will argue that participation in the arts is an expression of the *imago Dei* and that as individuals create or encounter art, they are formed and transformed into the fullness of this cruciform identity. First, I will identify and address the theological concerns that have been raised regarding the use of the arts in Christian formation within the history of the Reformed tradition. Second, I will argue for the pedagogical value of the inclusion of the arts for Christian formation from a theological perspective. Third, I will argue that participation in the arts is a uniquely human activity and as such is an expression of the *imago Dei*. Finally, I will put these theologically normative claims in dialogue with the claim made by young adults that the arts foster connection, expression, and opening within their faith lives. This is in service to my overarching argument that participation in the arts functions as theologically rich practical reason wherein the Christian identity of young adults is transformed through fellowship (connection), vulnerably sharing their beliefs and identity (expression), and an exocentric orientation to the world and God (opening).

The first section will rehearse the writings of John Calvin and Karl Barth regarding the pedagogical and theological advantages and dangers of using the arts for practices of Christian education and formation. Their concerns are legitimate for any time, and especially during the time in which they wrote. By identifying and heeding these warnings, I will move forward to suggest a positive role for the arts in the faith lives of young adults.

The second section will engage the work of John Dillenberger to make an epistemological argument for the inclusion of the arts within theological education. Even though Dillenberger wrote for theological education at the graduate level, his argument regarding theological epistemology translates well into practices of Christian education and formation with young adults.

The third section will engage the work of Wentzel van Huyssteen. In *Alone in the World?* Van Huyssteen claims that the creation of artwork is a form of symbolic communication that is a uniquely human activity. As such, it is an expression of the *imago Dei* that connects humans to one another while engaging the religious imagination in order to open up humanity to possibilities within and beyond the world.[1]

The final section will consider the theological claims of young adults through the normative lens provided by Van Huyssteen, which defines human uniqueness as the *imago Dei* and finds evidence of its expression in the arts. These theological claims will be considered both as they are explicitly and implicitly present in the statements of young adults.

A HISTORICAL SKETCH OF THEOLOGICAL AND PEDAGOGICAL CONCERNS

Reformed theologians John Calvin and Karl Barth had a variety of concerns about the arts, many of them related to practices of Christian education and formation. Their concerns have included distraction, idolatry, spiritual immaturity, misrepresentation, and poor stewardship of money. All are legitimate and serve as warnings for the contemporary context. They have also identified great potential for the arts, including their ability to aid individuals in understanding divine things on a deeper level, to make learning more interesting and accessible, and to draw attention to God's beautiful and creative work within the world. Both Calvin and Barth offer warnings about the arts, aware of their powerful potential for formation and therefore malformation.

---

1. Van Huyssteen, *Alone in the World?*

Calvin and Barth have been selected because they represent a distinct line of theological argumentation within the Reformed tradition. In order to present their thoughts in a digestible form I have used a two-part framework for looking at their claims. First, I will consider their claims regarding the pedagogical use of the arts for the purposes of Christian formation. Second, I will consider the theological claims they make concerning art and Christian formation.

John Calvin (1509–64)

Pedagogical Concerns: Knowledge of the Arts May Aid in Deeper Spiritual Knowledge

John Calvin opened his *Institutes* by stating that as humanity reflects upon itself, it is provoked to seek after knowledge of the divine. In Calvin's words, "the knowledge of ourselves" that we gain through contemplation of and interaction with the world "not only arouses us to seek God, but also, as it were, leads us by the hand to find him."[2] Self-knowledge, especially in relation to uniquely human capacities (such as the ability to create and engage art), can potentially lead to knowledge of God. The natural world, too, displays the "divine wisdom" that makes the revelation of God's glory accessible to all. Calvin wrote,

> There are innumerable evidences both in heaven and on earth that declare his wonderful wisdom; not only those more recondite matters for the closer observation of which astronomy, medicine, and all natural science are intended, but also those which thrust themselves upon the sight of even the most untutored and ignorant persons, so that they cannot open their eyes without being compelled to witness them.[3]

He went on to say, "Indeed, men who have either quaffed or even tasted the liberal arts penetrate with their aid far more deeply into the secrets of the divine wisdom."[4] These statements suggest that Calvin believed that the liberal arts were tools that could aid an individual in knowing God and theological truths more deeply.

---

2. Calvin, *Institutes*, I.1.1.
3. Calvin, *Institutes*, I.1.2.
4. Calvin, *Institutes*, I.5.2.

There was, however, a problem. Despite the grand witness of the theater of creation, both within humanity and within the world, human sin was blinding and pervasive, and therefore "the manifestation of God in nature speaks to us in vain."[5] In light of this reality, "Scripture is needed as guide and teacher for anyone who would come to God the Creator."[6] Calvin claimed that "with the aid of spectacles" humanity was able to see God and God's work in the world.[7] These spectacles consist of Scripture, which helps us in "gathering up the otherwise confused knowledge of God in our minds, having dispersed our dullness."[8] When worn they "clearly show us the true God."[9] These spectacles provide us with knowledge of what the kingdom of God is like, and therefore, when we see redemption happening that resonates with the kingdom, we are able to name it as such. The converse is also true. Without Scripture as a lens through which to view the world, it is not possible to identify the redemptive and transformative work of God, because it is unrecognizable to one who is unaware of God's revelation in Scripture. According to Calvin, Scripture does not speak alone but relies on the inner testimony of the Holy Spirit.

In a section titled "The witness of the Holy Spirit: This is stronger than all proof," Calvin claimed that "we ought to seek our conviction in a higher place than human reasons, judgments, or conjectures, that is, in the secret testimony of the Spirit."[10] Not wanting to rely upon rational proofs for God, Calvin landed on an experiential argument for revelation. Scripture is needed as a guide and teacher. Additionally, it provides the spectacles through which humanity may interpret the glory of God found in the natural world. The strongest proof for humanity—stronger than Scripture or reason—was the inner conviction of the Holy Spirit mysteriously self-revealed within the lives of individuals. Calvin described this as "a feeling that can be born only of heavenly revelation. I speak of nothing other than what each believer experiences within himself—though my words fall far beneath a just explanation of the matter."[11] This beautiful section of the *Institutes* exposes

---

5. Calvin, *Institutes*, I.5.14.

6. Calvin, *Institutes*, I.6.1.

7. Calvin, *Institutes*, I.6.1.

8. Calvin, *Institutes*, I.6.1.

9. Calvin, *Institutes*, I.6.1.

10. Calvin, *Institutes*, I.7.4.

11. Calvin, *Institutes*, I.7.5.

the limitations of human reason, leaving "each believer" with "a feeling" and "experiences within himself" as the core of their faith.[12]

The freedom of the Holy Spirit to convict believers is truly free, and this means that revelation can occur through any medium, including the arts and even artists. John de Gruchy highlights places in the *Institutes* where Calvin linked the creative work of humanity to the work of the Holy Spirit. According to Calvin, "The Holy Spirit was the source of genuine artistic creativity, and artistic gifts sometimes flowered more brilliantly among those who were not believers. All arts, sculpture and painting amongst them, come from God and bring pleasure."[13]

As de Gruchy rightly points out, Calvin credited God as the creative source behind the arts by giving creation the ability to create. Despite this positive disposition toward the arts, Calvin never took the next step to propose how, when, or to what end people should engage the arts.[14] He did, however, go to great lengths to explain how and when they should not be used.

Theological Concerns: Idolatry

Despite his acknowledgment that artistic ability was a gift from God, Calvin was deeply concerned with images and their potential to tempt individuals into idolatry, especially when the subject of the art was God. This concern garnered significant attention during the Reformation and continues to be a topic of discussion within the realm of theological aesthetics for Reformed theologians today. In a chapter titled "It Is Unlawful to Attribute a Visible Form to God, and Generally Whoever Sets Up Idols Revolts Against the True God," Calvin directly addressed the use of images to depict God, as well as their use in worship. His section titles alone clearly stated his argument.[15]

12. Calvin, *Institutes*.

13. De Gruchy, *Christianity, Art and Transformation*, 43, citing Calvin, *Institutes*, I.11.12 and II.2.16.

14. In a section on the role and value of teachers, Calvin claimed that God accommodates to human ways of knowing, and one way that God does this is by using teachers. I believe this is true not only relationally (i.e., we learn from other people) but also aesthetically (i.e., God accommodates to our learning needs through various media such as the arts). Calvin, *Institutes*, 4.1.4.

15. "1. We are forbidden every pictorial representation of God"; "2. Every figurative representation of God contradicts his being"; "3. Even direct signs of the divine Presence give no justification for images"; "4. Images and pictures are contrary to Scripture." Calvin, *Institutes*, I.11.

His line of argumentation was rooted in his concern that humanity is prone to making idols out of the created world, confusing them with God. Referring to the pervasiveness of sin, which incites the human desire to worship anything, especially idols of their own making, Calvin wrote,

> Since this brute stupidity gripped the whole world—to pant after visible figures of God, and thus to form gods of wood, stone, gold, silver, or other dead and corruptible matter—we must cling to this principle: God's glory is corrupted by an impious falsehood whenever any form is attached to him. Therefore in the law, after having claimed for himself alone the glory of deity, when he would teach what worship he approves or repudiates, God soon adds, "You shall not make for yourself a graven image, nor any likeness" [Exod 20:4]. By these words he restrains our waywardness from trying to represent him by any visible image, and briefly enumerates all those forms by which superstition long ago began to turn truth into falsehood.[16]

Here Calvin directly connected the creation of images of God with the second commandment. Calvin was aware of those who held a position that allowed for greater accommodation and addressed them directly. He challenged Pope Gregory's median way, saying, "I know that it is pretty much an old saw that images are the books of the uneducated. Gregory said this; yet the Spirit of God declares far otherwise; if Gregory had been taught in His school with regard to this, he never would have spoken thus."[17] He went

---

16. Calvin, *Institutes*, 1.11.1.

17. Calvin, *Institutes*, 1.11.5. Pope Gregory the Great has regularly been cited as advocating for a moderate stance with regard to the arts in response to the iconoclasts. In a letter to Serenus, bishop of Massilia (Marseilles), he wrote, "We commend you for your zeal against anything made by hand being an object of adoration, but we declare that you should not have destroyed these images. Pictures are used in churches for this reason: that those who are ignorant of letters may at least read what they cannot read in books by looking at the walls. Therefore, my brother, you should have preserved the images and at the same time have prohibited the people from worshiping them." Gregory's admonition to preserve the arts for the illiterate has been quoted throughout history and was highly influential for those writing on images in the medieval and Reformed period. To have paintings and images depicting God and biblical scenes was a low form of initial pedagogy that Pope Gregory supported. Theologically, this statement exposes Gregory's awareness of the difference between accommodation to learning needs and idolatry. According to Gregory, the iconoclasts made a pedagogical error in removing one resource for learning within the church. Theologically, however, Gregory supported the iconoclasts' zeal to combat idolatry, even while he questioned their methods. Gregory the Great, *Selected Epistles*, quoted in Brown, *Good Taste, Bad Taste, and Christian Taste*, 33.

on to further critique the papists, saying that had they taught the correct doctrine from the start, the "uneducated" would never have needed images as an aid in the first place. Calvin rebuked those who failed in their duties to teach the young and the illiterate because their failure positioned people to worship idols. What Calvin found even more reprehensible was that they made pedagogical arguments to justify their laziness. Addressing this situation he said, "Whoever, therefore, desires to be rightly taught must learn what he should know of God from some other source than images."[18] Calvin's zeal against images was in order to adhere to the second commandment and had the consequence of distinguishing a Reformed way of worship from a Roman Catholic form. The distinguishing features of a Reformed way were not only theological in an abstract sense but, as is evident here, included aesthetic choices as well.

According to Calvin, one of the effects of sin was the human proclivity for making idols. He explained, "The mind begets an idol; the hand gives it birth."[19] His main concern was with the veneration of images and the superstitious practices surrounding images or sometimes even consecrated places within the Roman Catholic Church.[20] Despite this, Calvin differentiated between the making of art generally and the making of art that sought to represent God. He wrote,

> And yet, I am not gripped by the superstition of thinking absolutely no images permissible. But because sculpture and painting are gifts of God, I seek a pure and legitimate use of each, lest those things which the Lord has conferred upon us for his glory and our good be not only polluted by perverse misuse but also turned to our destruction.[21]

According to Calvin, a pure and legitimate use would be to paint or sculpt only those things "which the eyes are capable of seeing."[22] Even with this qualification, however, he still believed "that even if the use of images contained nothing evil, it still has no value for teaching."[23] We must assume he meant teaching within the context of worship because of his affirmation

---

18. Calvin, *Institutes*, 1.11.6.

19. Calvin, *Institutes*, 1.11.8.

20. Calvin, *Institutes*, 1.11.9.

21. Calvin, *Institutes*, 1.11.12.

22. Calvin, *Institutes*, 1.11.12.

23. Calvin, *Institutes*.

of the liberal arts and their ability to help individuals understand divine wisdom more deeply, as noted above.

In an appeal to tradition, to add support to his theological argument from Scripture, Calvin claimed that no images, regardless of content, were appropriate in churches. He referenced the first five hundred years of Christianity, claiming that it was a time when the church flourished without any images.[24] Clearly, this is an overstatement that historians and archeologists have disproved, but it exposes his concern that the church has strayed from its original aesthetic. Ultimately, Calvin believed that creative ability and artmaking were indeed gifts from God; however, their proper use was outside of the church and their proper content was the natural, visible world and not the divine, invisible God.

Karl Barth (1886–1968)

Pedagogical Concerns: The Arts Misrepresent and Distract

Barth had numerous concerns with art. First, any attempt to portray God would always fail and end in imperfection. He wrote,

> No human art should try to represent—in their unity—the suffering God and triumphant man, the beauty of God which is the beauty of Jesus Christ. If at this point we have one urgent request to all Christian artists, however well-intentioned, gifted or even possessed of genius, it is that they should give up this unholy undertaking—for the sake of God's beauty. This picture, the one true picture, both in object and representation, cannot be copied, for the express reason that it speaks for itself, even in its beauty.[25]

The misrepresentation of God is attached to Barth's pedagogical concern regarding what people imagine God to be or look like. If people are exposed to only one image, for example, they may consciously or unconsciously assume that this image is what God looks like.

Barth was also concerned that images in church distracted individuals from listening to the preached word. According to Barth, artistic representations of Jesus compete with preaching. Interpreting this move using pedagogical categories, the implicit curriculum (images) was competing

---

24. Calvin, *Institutes*, 1.11.12.

25. Barth, *Church Dogmatics*, II/1:666.

with the explicit curriculum (preaching). Both have the power to teach; however, Barth clearly prioritized the preached word. He wrote,

> This decisive task of preaching in divine service seems to suggest that the presence of artistic representations of Jesus Christ is not desirable in the places of assembly. For it is almost inevitable that such static works should constantly attract the eye and therefore the conscious or unconscious attention of the listening community, fixing them upon the particular conception of Jesus Christ entertained in all good faith no doubt by the artist. This is suspect for two reasons. *The community should not be bound to a particular conception, as inevitably happens where there is an artistic representation*, but should be led by the ongoing proclamation of His History as His History with us, so that it moves from one provisional Amen to another, in the wake of His living self-attestation pressing on from insight to insight. Supremely, however, *even the most excellent of plastic arts does not have the means to display Jesus in His truth*, i.e., in His unity as true Son of God and Son of Man.[26]

In addition to his acknowledgment that images have the power to form beliefs about God, Barth rightly identifies the human limitation of the artist to display Jesus Christ in all of his fullness. He was wary that artists would never quite portray God correctly. He wrote, "There will necessarily be either on the one side, as in the great Italians, an abstract and docetic overemphasis on His deity, or on the other, as in Rembrandt, an equally abstract, ebionite overemphasis on His humanity, so that even with the best of intentions error will be promoted."[27] In this desperate situation, Barth proposed, "If we certainly cannot prevent artists from attempting this exciting and challenging theme, it should at least be made clear both to them and to the community that it is better not to allow works of this kind to compete with the ministry of preaching."[28] It seems right to assume here that he would be in agreement with Calvin that the appropriate place for images is outside of the church. Barth's pedagogical concerns are deeply theological as well.

---

26. Barth, *Church Dogmatics*, IV.3.2:868. Emphasis mine.
27. Barth, *Church Dogmatics*, IV.3.2:868.
28. Barth, *Church Dogmatics*, IV.3.2:868.

Theological Concerns: Misrepresenting God

In the references above it is clear that Barth was theologically concerned that artists would misrepresent God and then their image of God would be malformed. The assumption here, and with Calvin as well, was that God is abstract and invisible (with the exception of Jesus, whom we have no pictorial record of), and any attempt to make God concrete and visible would inevitably fail and lead astray. The Italian and Dutch painters who overemphasized either the divinity or the humanity of Jesus exemplify his concerns. There is also an assumption that any image of God will almost always immediately cause humans to swoon into a state of false devotion, either consciously or subconsciously worshipping the image before them. Despite his theological and pedagogical concerns, it is well known that Barth loved the music of Mozart and commented theologically on the Isenheim Altarpiece, which captivated his imagination.[29] What is most fascinating, perhaps, about Barth and Calvin is how they both appreciate and reject the arts.

A PEDAGOGICAL ARGUMENT FOR THE VALUE OF THE ARTS FOR PRACTICES OF CHRISTIAN FORMATION

Having served as president of the American Academy of Religion, as well as academic dean and president of Graduate Theological Union, John Dillenberger (1918–2008) played a unique role within the contemporary discussion regarding the use of the arts in Christian education and formation. He was trained as a historian with a focus on the arts. With respect to theological education for seminary students, Dillenberger argued that a full epistemology was at stake regarding the inclusion or exclusion of the arts in theological education. During his tenure at Graduate Theological Union he sought to implement these convictions. Given his roles it is obvious that his writing was for seminary students; however, I believe his argument naturally translates into practices of Christian education and formation for young adults.

The final chapter of Dillenberger's book *A Theology of Artistic Sensibilities: The Visual Arts and the Church* is titled "Theological Education and the Reappropriation of the Visual."[30] In this final chapter, Dillenberger

29. Gill, "Barth and Mozart," 403–11; Milliner, "A Vacation for Grünewald."

30. Dillenberger, *A Theology of Artistic Sensibilities*, 250.

argued that the arts are a medium of knowledge, just like language, and therefore expand the possibilities of theological epistemology. His main claim was that the arts and the visual world were a medium containing knowledge, and so to ignore what can be taught and learned through a medium other than language is to ignore one dimension of the epistemic ability of humans.

The Arts and Theological Education

Dillenberger claimed that theological education has tended to focus on the mind and spirit—that is, the cognitive and ethereal dimensions of the Christian life rather than the embodied dimensions.[31] To shift to a wholistic educational model, he argued, theological education must include the visual and aesthetic in order to encompass the full epistemological capability of humanity.[32] Dillenberger's work was on visual art, and so he makes this argument for the visual arts; however, this line of argumentation can easily be expanded to include the full range of artistic experiences.

Just as the mind should be cultivated to argue rationally, within the rules of a language world, Dillenberger asserted,

> Seeing has its own discipline, born of continuous seeing. Such seeing organizes the world in its own manner. Seeing as such, like talk as such, requires habituated effort. Only a concern with seeing will restore sight to its rightful place.
>
> It is one of the ironies of Western history that the emphasis on religion and Christianity as a matter of the spirit—a phraseology that itself inverts the notion that spirit is expressed through matter—has a tinge of otherworldliness that leaves the world aesthetically untouched. It is surprising, however, that such a religion of spirit frequently leads to social and political involvements. Aesthetic dimensions, when present at all, are accidental, like frosting on the cake. That is what happens when seeing is relegated to what bombards us, when seeing is not a cultivated sorting-out of impressions or a forming of reality through sight.[33]

31. The following books reveal a renewed focus on practices; however, these have not given sustained attention to either the arts or young adults. Bass, *Receiving the Day*; Bass, *Practicing Our Faith*; Dykstra, *Growing in the Life of Faith*; Smith and Smith, *Teaching and Christian Practices*.

32. Dillenberger, *Theology of Artistic Sensibilities*, 251.

33. Dillenberger, *Theology of Artistic Sensibilities*, 251.

This argument for the cultivation of seeing as a discipline might be made for bodily interaction, hearing, tasting, and perhaps even smelling as well. Dillenberger suggested that all of the traditional disciplines within the seminary would benefit from increased appropriation of the arts within their field, enriching their curriculum and exposing their own limitations. Ultimately, his claim and critique was that words cannot say all there is to be said, taught, or known. This is true not only for the education of seminarians and divinity students but for everyone.

The Arts in Congregational Life

Dillenberger also commented on the arts in congregational life. He claimed that the "new interest in spirituality and the renewed interest in liturgy disclose a longing of the human spirit for experiences that are more than exercises in thought."[34] His insight, originally written in 1986, has been borne out throughout the 1990s and today. In his more recent research, Robert Wuthnow found a similar desire within congregations and interpreted the meaning of this for ministers, writing,

> Religious leaders need to understand the profound cultural shift that the current interest in the arts represents. It is a move away from cognition and thus from knowledge and belief, a move toward experience and toward a more complete integration of the senses into the spiritual life. It is uncharted territory. Few clergy have learned anything in seminary that will help them to address it.[35]

There has been an increased interest in aesthetically rich liturgical resources within the Reformed tradition; however, this has not fully moved into the realm of Christian education and formation. Dillenberger suggested the use of visual arts for individual and congregationally led meditation. He wrote,

> Surely meditation can be facilitated by objects as well as by verbal or nonverbal directives . . . An art object or a stained-glass window, whether in a simple service or a liturgical extravaganza, can become a point of attention in which meditation, instruction, or edification may occur.[36]

---

34. Dillenberger, *Theology of Artistic Sensibilities*, 253.

35. Wuthnow, *All in Sync*, 245.

36. Dillenberger, *Theology of Artistic Sensibilities*, 254.

This edification includes not only personal spiritual growth but also the ability to attend to those who are different. The practice of meditation and self-conscious interpretation is a skill that can be taught. Dillenberger claimed that cultivating the ability to attend to artwork gives individuals the practice and tools to engage with others in their difference. In his words, "The stretching of our sensibilities is necessary if we are to understand and come to terms with our pluralistic world."[37] He roots the connection between individuals on our common humanity.[38]

The Arts in Christian Formation

In addition to these claims from Dillenberger, I also believe that the arts foster shared vulnerability along with increased self-awareness regarding interpretive choices and one's own hermeneutical lens. The arts are also valuable because they naturally embrace mystery and nuance, both of which are dimensions of a life of faith. Finally, the arts make learning enjoyable.

Pedagogues such as bell hooks and Jack Mezirow claim that when individuals are vulnerable they are most open to learning and being transformed.[39] For hooks, vulnerability is cultivated within the classroom, through relationships that seek to transgress the traditional roles of teacher and student.[40] For Mezirow, vulnerability occurs in disorienting dilemmas wherein individuals are brought up short due to lack of knowledge or experience.[41] In addition to these, I believe that vulnerability happens as individuals share their creation for others to encounter. Cultivating an atmosphere of shared vulnerability invites greater self-awareness with regard to both one's ontology and epistemology. Vulnerability is both allowing yourself to be known by another and the inward turn to knowing yourself.

Recently I taught a freshman course in which a young woman (not a particapant in this study) shared a banner she had made for her high school. This was a part of a presentation she gave to address the question, Who are

---

37. Dillenberger, *Theology of Artistic Sensibilities*, 256.

38. Like Dewey, he said that there was something about the arts that unites humanity. This common desire, I believe, is the exocentric impulse within humanity that will be explained below.

39. hooks, *Teaching to Transgress*; Mezirow, *Transformative Dimensions of Adult Learning*.

40. hooks, *Teaching to Transgress*, 13–22.

41. Mezirow, *Transformative Dimensions of Adult Learning*, 150–60.

your people? On the banner was painted a World War II–era plane dropping bombs, with the word "Bombers" across the top. Her hometown was Hanford, Washington, where the nuclear bombs dropped during World War II were produced. Hanford is currently the most contaminated nuclear waste site in the United States. Using PowerPoint the young woman displayed an image of the banner and described how hard it was to paint and how big it was when they hung it up. It was obvious that she was proud of this banner, which displayed her artistic skill as well as hometown pride. At one point she turned and saw the reaction of her classmates, then looked back at the screen, and then had a very public moment of self-awareness: after a brief pause she said, "I guess it's kind of messed up that we are proud of being the Bombers." Moments of insight like this—when art speaks back to its maker, when we see our hometown in a new way or suddenly we are able to see ourselves through the eyes of another—these moments happen when we are able to share vulnerably with others. Moments of vulnerability such as this one provide young adults with space to be transformed.

In a postmodern age the ability to embrace a multitude of interpretations as "right" or "true" is increasingly not only welcome but also valued as an interpretive skill. The arts—by presenting ideas, knowledge, truth claims, and protests in a symbolic medium—are able to embody the nuanced dimensions of a message—what Paul Ricoeur would call a "surplus of meaning."[42] Words and language have this potential as well, although I believe this surplus is most evident to those engaged in the act of interpreting non-linguistic forms of communication.

Finally, the arts make learning (and growing in faith) enjoyable. Joy is a real thing with real effects on motivation, retention, and investment. As remarked on in chapter 3, play is the natural disposition of humanity toward the world to learn.[43]

---

42. Ricoeur, *Interpretation Theory*, 55.

43. I am very interested in play and learning theory, and while I have not given sustained attention to this here, I intend to do so in future work by engaging with the following writers on the topic. Berryman, *Godly Play*; Brown and Vaughan, *Play: How It Shapes the Brain, Opens the Imagination, and Invigorates the Soul*; Goto, "Artistic Play: Seeking the God of the Unexpected"; Piaget, *Play, Dreams and Imitation in Childhood*; Vygotsky, *Mind in Society*.

A THEOLOGICAL ARGUMENT FOR THE ARTS AS AN EXPRESSION OF THE IMAGO DEI

The work of Wentzel van Huyssteen will now be engaged in order to argue that participation in the arts is a uniquely human activity and is therefore an expression of the *imago Dei*. I will argue with van Huyssteen that artmaking is one expression of the *imago Dei* as it embodies the exocentric orientation of humanity that desires to record and interpret life events as well as communicate with others. All of this is in service to my overarching argument that participation in the arts can function as theologically rich practical reason wherein the Christian identity of young adults is transformed.

In *Alone in the World?* van Huyssteen engages in an interdisciplinary dialogue between theology and Paleolithic anthropology to argue for a shared understanding of human uniqueness. He comes to agreement between these fields on the unique capacity of humanity to make art. Unlike the rest of creation, humans seek out meaning to both guide and understand their life experience.[44] The medium of this meaning-making is the creation of culture, one form of which is art. Van Huyssteen uses Philip Hefner's definition of culture: "the behaviors we humans choose, together with the interpretations by which we give meaning and justification to those behaviors."[45] Culture includes the rituals, artifacts, language, and symbol systems that give meaning to human life.

The theological language for human uniqueness is the *imago Dei*. Van Huyssteen rehearses the trajectory of theological writing on the *imago Dei*, exposing a movement from being defined as the disembodied soul that seeks dominion over the creation to an embodied, relational definition under the influence of contemporary feminist insights.[46] Evidence of the *imago Dei* can be seen in the human attempt to communicate, interpret, and record human experience through the making of culture.

Van Huyssteen connects the human impulse to make culture to Wolfhart Pannenberg's definition of the *imago Dei*. Pannenberg argued that humanity has the identity of the *imago Dei* both by virtue of creation (Gen 1:26; Ps 8:5ff) and by destiny through our transformation into the likeness of Jesus Christ (Rom 8:29; 1 Cor 15:49; 2 Cor 3:18). He explained,

---

44. Van Huyssteen, *Alone in the World?*, 148.

45. Van Huyssteen, *Alone in the World?*, 148.

46. Van Huussteen, *Alone in the World?*, 116–58.

In Paul's sayings about Christ as the image of God into which all others must be transformed, the Christian doctrine of the divine likeness must see an elucidation of our general destiny of divine likeness. But in so doing it may not expunge the differences between the fulfilling of our divine likeness in and by Jesus Christ on the one hand, and the OT statements about Adam's divine likeness on the other. To do this is to miss the point that our destiny as creatures is brought to fulfillment by Jesus Christ.[47]

Pannenberg explained that various theologians, such as Irenaeus, have attempted to resolve this tension by claiming that our likeness to God is by degree. Pannenberg argued that this was not correct; humanity was never the perfect *imago Dei*, but always lacking, even before the entrance of sin into the world. In making this argument, he reserved a place for Jesus Christ as the true *imago Dei*. He wrote, "Only in Jesus, as Christian anthropology sees it, did the image of God appear with full clarity." In the story of the human race, then, the image of God was not achieved fully at the outset. It was still in process. This is true not only of the likeness but of the image itself. But since likeness is essential to an image, our creation in the image of God stands implicitly related to full similarity. This full actualization is our destiny, one that was historically achieved with Jesus Christ and in which others may participate by transformation into the image of Christ.

Pannenberg connected human longing for transformation into the likeness of Christ with the exocentric impulse, or *Weltoffenheit*, meaning openness to the world and beyond the world. Humanity longs for the full actualization of its destiny, which is life with God as the Father has life with the Son.

As the created image of God, humanity longs for fellowship. Humanity does not merely desire fellowship but is created with an orientation for fellowship. Pannenberg made this argument by building on Karl Barth's claim in *Church Dogmatics* III/2 that humanity was created for "life with God."[48] Pannenberg explained,

> If our destiny is set with our creation in the divine image so that descriptions of it must be oriented to the implications of the relation of the image to God, then from the very first as God's creatures we are destined for fellowship with God, for "life with God." The point of likeness to God is fellowship with him . . . This condition

47. Pannenberg, *Systematic Theology*, 2:210.
48. Barth, *Church Dogmatics*, III/2:1.

concerns not only our relation to God but also our relation to others since humanity as a whole, and not just this or that individual, is destined for fellowship with God.[49]

The condition of longing after, and orientation toward, life with God is the mark of the image of God. Pannenberg identified two dimensions of the *imago Dei*—humanity's current state as created in the image of God and humanity's future destiny as being like Christ, who is the image of God. He described humanity's created state as a copy of the original—the image of God within humanity is a copy of God, who is the original.

To fulfill their destiny, humanity must be like Christ. Connecting the Apostle Paul's claims with the creation narrative, Pannenberg wrote, "If our creation in the divine image implies our destiny of fellowship with the eternal God, then the incarnation of God in Jesus of Nazareth may be seen as a fulfillment of this destiny."[50] He explained further, "We must think of the life of the creature as inwardly moved by its divine destiny, even though, for reasons yet to be discussed, the fulfillment of the destiny did not take place at the beginning of human history but will come only as the goal and consummation of this history."[51] The *imago Dei* in the interim seeks out fellowship, or connection, with God as well as the rest of humanity. The *imago Dei* is marked by *Weltoffenheit* in an effort both to know and to be known. Significant for this research is the intrinsic longing within humanity to fulfill its destiny—which is present, yet incomplete—as the *imago Dei*. The search for completion takes the form of a search for fellowship with God and with the rest of humanity who share a similar restless longing. We see this longing within the artistic lives of young adults.

Pannenberg identified this restlessness within humanity as having qualities of both dissatisfaction and hope. He wrote,

> We are the theme of a history in which we become what we already are. At present the goal is indistinct. It is not even present to us as a goal but only in an indefinite trust that opens up the horizon of world experience and intersubjectivity, and also in a restless thrust toward overcoming the finite . . . It also gives evidence of a knowledge that the final horizon in which we see the true meaning of the data of life transcends the whole compass of the finite.[52]

49. Pannenberg, *Systematic Theology*, 2:224.

50. Pannenberg, Systematic Theology, 2:225.

51. Pannenberg, *Systematic Theology*, 2:227.

52. Pannenberg, *Systematic Theology*, 2:228–29.

This dissatisfaction includes the current finite problems that are the result of sin in the world, as well as an orientation toward the infinite in the form of hope in the coming of the kingdom of God. Humanity does not merely resign itself to living with this restlessness but attempts to relieve it through changing the finite world and *Weltoffenheit* for what God might be doing in the present. Pannenberg would identify this movement within the world as the coming of the kingdom of God. Ultimately, Pannenberg claimed that "only by accepting our finitude as God-given do we attain to the fellowship with God that is implied in our destiny of divine likeness. In other words, we must be fashioned into the image of the Son, of his self-distinction from the Father. We participate thus in the fellowship of the Son with the Father."[53]

In Pannenberg's anthropology it is this disposition for fellowship that is reinterpreted as our final destiny, which theologically is manifested already in Jesus Christ and in which believers already share through the power of the Spirit, and thus already is effecting the eschatological reality of the new human being in them.

The true identity of humanity is only found and known in the person of Jesus Christ. The relationship between the Son and the Father is the model for human fellowship with God. This includes a self-awareness of one's finitude in relationship to God. Jesus' relationship with humanity is the model for human relationships as one that is centered on God. As those conferred with the *imago Dei* through creation, humanity lives in a state of real fellowship with God and the rest of humanity, as well as having a restless longing and *Weltoffenheit*. While awaiting and anticipating its destiny, humanity seeks fellowship, relationships, and meaningful interpretations of life. The actualization of real fellowship with God and others happens through the power of the Holy Spirit and is the eschatological reality of the anticipated kingdom of God.

Using this definition of the *imago Dei* from Pannenberg, van Huyssteen argues that the *imago Dei* is manifest in the human impulse and capacity to make art and, in doing so, self-consciously reflect upon human existence.[54] Van Huyssteen calls this impulse "the naturalness of religious imagination," which is found in humanity alone and distinguishes it from other living things.[55] He identifies "the imagination, productivity, and creativity" as "a

53. Pannenberg, *Systematic Theology*, 2:230.
54. Van Huyssteen, *Alone in the World?*, 268.
55. Van Huyssteen, *Alone in the World?*.

product of language, which makes language and symbolic abilities central to a definition of embodied human uniqueness."[56] Imagining something and then creating it through a symbolic or linguistic medium is an exocentric activity.[57] Using Pannenberg's understanding of exocentricity and *Weltoffenheit*, van Huyssteen explains,

> Exocentricity not only points to a human orientation to others and to the world, but in a much more holistic sense reveals a disposition of human nature itself. Humans have this *Weltoffenheit*, or openness to the world, which by far transcends the openness of all animals to their environment . . . Exocentricity thus means that humans are always open beyond every experience and beyond any given situation, in fact beyond the world itself. We are even open beyond our own cultural constructions: as we transform nature into culture, and constantly replace earlier forms of culture with new ones, we are also open beyond culture to the future, and to our finding our ultimate destiny in the future. This restlessness of human nature forms an important root for all religious life.[58]

The human impulse to make and create art for understanding and guidance is a theologically loaded activity, as it exposes the created disposition of humanity as the *imago Dei*. As van Huyssteen explains, the human search for meaningful interpretations of the world additionally exposes restlessness within humanity, which takes the form of existential questioning, wondering, and pondering in a disposition of openness toward the future and fulfillment as well as openness to God.

Humanity is restless not only for meaningful interpretations of experience but also for a more fundamental and deeper meaning to frame all of life. All of humanity is and will be restless until it realizes its destiny in likeness to Jesus Christ, who is the true *imago Dei* and the definition of what it means to be human. Van Huyssteen explains the tension between what it means to be created as the *imago Dei* and destined to be the *imago Dei*, saying,

---

56. Van Huyssteen, *Alone in the World?*, 231.

57. In her work *The Mind of the Maker*, Dorothy Sayers used a Trinitarian framework for understanding the work of the Holy Spirit as the idea, the energy, and the power to do creative work. Jürgen Moltmann is another theologian who emphasizes the relational dimension of the Trinity through the notion of perichoresis. See Moltmann, *The Trinity and the Kingdom*.

58. Van Huyssteen, *Alone in the World?*, 139–40.

For Pannenberg, in tightening his argument theologically, this fundamental self-transcendence and relationality of all humans to the future ultimately finds its proper identity in Jesus Christ, who fulfills the image of God in its entirety. Theologically, therefore, we find our true identity, as well as the foundation for our relationships with others, in a relationality that is centered on God.[59]

The exocentric impulse within humanity that longs for fellowship and connection, both with God and with the rest of humanity, ultimately seeks to reflect the relationship between the Father and the Son, who are in perfect fellowship. Human attempts to connect with others and interpret life are evidence of the restless longing for the fulfillment of the *imago Dei* to become like Jesus Christ.

59. Van Huyssteen, *Alone in the World?*, 141.

5

AN AESTHETIC PRACTICAL THEOLOGY
OF YOUNG ADULT FAITH

One of the ways the Christian identity of young adults is formed and transformed is through participation in the arts. Their artmaking or artistic participation provides a medium through which they are able to express their unique identity. This activity fosters fellowship by connecting them with others and God. Their artmaking also exposes both restlessness and openness. Their openness is toward fellowship with God as well as others, specifically, the worship and devotional practices of others. Young adults also claimed that the arts were a medium where they could ponder or wrestle with existential questions that they had and also open up to God's presence in their life. As noted in the third chapter, many young adults identified the use of their unique artistic gifts as an expression of the *imago Dei* in a way that is resonant with van Huyssteen's claims.

Three themes emerge from this research and provide an aesthetic practical theology regarding the role of the arts within the faith lives of young adults. These three themes are relational—they are oriented toward fellowship with God or another person.

1. *Created and creative in the image of God*: The young adults in this study understand themselves to be a unique creation (some used the language of the *imago Dei*) gifted by God with unique artistic abilities.

2. *Incarnate intimacy*: The young adults in this study value and seek out relationships where they feel known. They value the way the arts foster connections between themselves and God, as well as others. They also valued the way the arts allowed for them to express their unique identity so that they might be known by others. These encounters are embodied and happen as they bodily interact with people, or the things other people have created.

3. *The creative presence of the Holy Spirit*: The young adults in this study believe that the Holy Spirit is active in their lives; they see this especially when they do activities that employ their creativity.

The relationship of these young adults to the triune God is both explicit and implicit. These young adults related to God explicitly through creation in the way that they talk about being uniquely gifted by God. They related to God through the incarnation implicitly with regard to an exocentric understanding of human identity as the *imago Dei*, which is oriented toward, and destined for, fellowship with God. Finally, these young adults relate to God through the Holy Spirit explicitly as they credit the Holy Spirit as the source who inspires creativity.

CREATED AND CREATIVE IN THE IMAGE OF GOD

The young adults in this study seem to have an impulse to create, to reflect upon creation, and to live in a way that is resonant with who God made them to be. This is seen when young adults claim that the arts allow for them to express their faith and their identity. There is an impulse toward living in resonance with one's unique, God-given identity. Theologically, van Huyssteen would identify this as the *imago Dei* as conferred upon humanity in creation. A young adult might claim, "Who God has made 'me' to be is who I am in my expressive actions. This 'me' is confirmed by others when they experience me and the things I make." Young adults are self-consciously aware that their gifts are unique ("no one can do *this* exactly the way I do it").

Young adults also believe that these unique abilities are gifts given by God. Their understanding of Christian identity is that they are uniquely created, made in the image of God, and one dimension of this means having unique, creative gifts. Young adults believe that these gifts from God are not given for personal enjoyment alone but are to be shared with the community.

Theologically, young adults claim that they have been made to create and share their unique contribution in the world. This notion of humanity as created by God and as possessing unique gifts that are to be shared is one dimension of forming a Christian identity. Individuals come to know who they are in relationship to the One who has made them. They are also formed as they share these gifts and receive the responses of others.

INCARNATE INTIMACY

Young adults desire to make things and participate in aesthetic events that go beyond themselves in a way that reaches out to others, both as they desire to be known and as they welcoming the beliefs and practices of others. Aesthetically rich activities communicate beliefs, values, and truths between people fostering connection and fellowship. This kind of boundary crossing can be seen in the openness of young adults to the aesthetic preferences and faith claims of others. Not only are they tolerant of other kinds of expression, but they promote it when it seems to encourage the faith of others.

The young adults in this study explicitly claimed that their creative gifts were a part of their identity as being created by God, and sometimes, and sometimes, they also connected this with creativity as one dimension of bearing the image of God. Van Huyssteen's claim challenges young adults to reflect upon the unrealized hope and future perfection of the *imago Dei* as fully revealed and actualized in the person of Jesus Christ. While young adults are aware of their identity in relationship to God, Pannenberg would claim that it is only fully realized when they find their true identity in the person of Jesus Christ. Until this moment, their restlessness might be interpreted as a restless longing for their destiny as the image of God in Jesus Christ.

THE CREATIVE PRESENCE OF THE HOLY SPIRIT

Young adults in this study believe that they have unique gifts from God and that the Holy Spirit works in their lives through the expression of these gifts. Just as the Greeks claimed that the muses inspired their creativity, so too, young adults claim a "muse" behind, within, and motivating their creative work. In the age of Moralistic Therapeutic Deism, when many young adults believe that God is a distant watchmaker, this awareness of holy and guiding presence is surprising and hopeful.[1] For these young adults, God is both the source and catalyst of creativity. What is unique to these Christian young adults, however, is that this activity is in line with the unique gifted-ness that God created them with.

CONCLUSION

In light of van Huyssteen's explanation of the *imago Dei* it is easy to see how the desire to express, connect, and open naturally happens during artistic participation. The category of exocentricity as a disposition of fellowship theologically frames these activities, so that they are not merely valuable but have a greater end, which is fellowship with others and the triune God—and, through this pursuit, transformation into the likeness of Jesus Christ. In this cycle of creation and self-reflection in relationship with others, Christian identity is formed (created) and transformed (re-created). This happens both as individuals reflect on who God has made them to be and as they experience the reactions of those who experience them. They are also formed as they seek to understand themselves (and their beliefs) in light of the beliefs of others. While young adults explicitly claim the exocentric value of the arts within their devotional life, they link this implicitly to the person of Jesus Christ, at best, or completely ignore it, at worst.

What is significant about these claims is twofold. First, the young adults in this study have a rich understanding of identity, calling, and gift-edness by God. They believe this about themselves as well as others. This calls them to embrace and accept otherness and difference. They see God at work not only in their own lives but also in the lives of others. There is a humility in this vision, as they do not claim to prescribe what the gifts of others are or how they should be used, even though many did say that gifts from God should be shared. Critics might say that this is postmodern pluralism at its worst; however, their claims were not an unqualified spiri-tuality of "do whatever works for you" but were rooted in the belief that God is free and humans are unique, and in the tension of this relationship literally anything could happen.

Second, there is a notable lack of diversity in the terms young adults use to refer to God (with "God" being the dominant term). Some did refer to Jesus, and a few more to the Holy Spirit, but they were not the majority. I wonder, however, if, given their proclivity toward openness, this is an effort

1. Smith, *Soul Searching*.

to be more inclusive toward the "God" of all creation, inclusive of those with religious views that are different from their own. This study did not look at pluralistic claims of young adults; however, it seems evident from what has been exposed here that young adults are very open to the beliefs of others— even non-Christian others. Participation in the arts made space for their own reflection upon their similarity to and difference from others and God. As they explained, this embodied practical reason, through aesthetic encounter, both forms and transforms their understanding of who they are.

Appendix A

The following letter is one example of the typical letter sent to young adults inviting them to participate in the study.

Hi [Name],

I got your name from [Name]. I am a PhD student at Princeton Theological Seminary, and I am doing a research project on young adults and the role that the arts play (if any) in their faith life. My study consists of two parts, interviews and a survey.

The online survey (linked below) takes about 15 to 20 minutes to fill out. I am looking to have as many young adults between the ages of 18 and 30 fill this out as possible. So if you would be willing to fill that out it would help me out a lot. If you wanted to forward this along to your friends that would be great! Upon completion you will have the chance to win a $100 gift card to amazon.com.

https://www.surveymonkey.com/s/faithandart

The second part is an interview. I am wondering if you would be willing to be interviewed over Skype (or over the phone) [or in person, if they live in New Jersey]. This would take about an hour. If so, reply to let me know.

Also, all of the information you provide will only be seen by me and will be reported anonymously. Thank you ahead of time for considering participating in this study!

Peace,
Katie Douglass

Appendix B

INTERVIEW GUIDE

Introduction to Project

- Katie Douglass, PhD candidate and PC(USA) minister, writing on young adults' faith practices.
- Explain how I found "you."
- Thank you for participating.

Primary Research Question: *What role does participation in the arts play in the devotional (or spiritual, or faith) lives of young adults?*

Church Involvement

1. How are you currently connected with the Presbyterian church?

    a. How were you connected in the past?

2. What is your interpretation of the PC(USA)'s view or position regarding the use of the arts in worship? In educational events?

3. What has been your experience of the arts in Presbyterian churches?

4. What church or religious events have you attended where you felt the presence of God? What were these like?

Aesthetic Practices

5. How do you currently participate in the arts? More than one way?

Arts and Spirituality

6. Is this participation a part of or an expression of your spiritual life?

7. Would you have made a connection between your faith and your artistic practices if I had not asked?

8. Do you have any beliefs about God that inform the way you think about the arts and spirituality?

Closing Questions

9. *What role does participation in the arts play in the devotional (or spiritual) lives of young adults?*

10. Is there anything else on any of these topics that you would like to tell me about?

Appendix C

OVERVIEW OF METHODS, SAMPLE SELECTION, AND SURVEY FINDINGS

In March 2011, I ran a test of the online survey in which twenty-four individuals took the survey, identifying functional or linguistic issues that were then corrected. Between April and November 2011, 492 individuals took the survey; 448 were between the ages of eighteen and thirty. Of these, 326 identified themselves as affiliated with the PC(USA) at one time or another through a PC(USA) ministry. Of these, 148 were raised in the PC(USA) and 142 currently identify as PC(USA). In order to get the results for my sample frame I ran a filter for individuals who were raised in the PC(USA) or who currently identified as PC(USA) and were between the ages of eighteen and thirty. This narrowed my sample to 176 individuals. All who were interviewed took the survey before we met. In total, thirty-four individuals were interviewed; however, four were eliminated from the sample because they did not completely match the sample frame. Despite their exclusion, their responses were complementary to the responses of the thirty interviewed.

The Internet link for the survey was dispersed in three ways: by email, over facebook.com, and through business cards with people that I met. I initially dispersed the link to the survey by emailing my friends, family, coworkers in ministry, professors, and classmates who forwarded the link along to their friends, family, and acquaintances. Additionally, as I traveled and spoke at various events throughout the spring, summer, and fall of 2011, I invited participants to share this link with individuals they knew who were between the ages of eighteen and thirty. This method of contact is called snowball sampling. As this link was shared, some recipients posted the link on Facebook, inviting their friends to take the survey. As a final step, I posted the link on my Facebook page as well. Finally, I made about 1500 "business cards" that included the link to the survey as well as my contact information. I handed these out everywhere I went, including a U2 concert in Philadelphia. These business cards included information about the incentive I added to the survey in July. This incentive was provided through Survey Monkey. I paid fifteen dollars to have my survey partici-pants entered in a chance to win a $100 gift card to amazon.com. One person was selected each week from all of the individuals participating in any of the currently active Survey Monkey surveys. The online surveying website surveymonkey.com was used.

COLLECTING RESEARCH PARTICIPANTS

As mentioned in chapter 3, some young adults were contacted for interview through the survey, two were individuals whom I knew before the study, and the rest of the contacts were made either through a mutual acquain-tance or a second or third degree of snowballing. Individuals confirmed that they were between the ages of eighteen and thirty and were also in some way, at some point, connected with the PC(USA). They were then contacted by email and asked to participate in a survey and interview.[1] I set up a time and place to meet with those who agreed to participate. For thirteen individuals this involved an in-person interview where we met at a neutral location such as a coffee shop or campus office. I asked them to select the meeting place, and if they were unsure of where to meet, I would offer options near the area they lived in. At most, I drove an hour to meet with someone for an interview. I always offered to buy them coffee; however, they always chose to purchase their own beverage. The seventeen interviews that were not done in person were conducted over Skype. For some, this was due to distance; for others who lived within a distance I was willing to drive, this was simply more convenient. For two of these, I called the individual's phone through Skype while they drove between their home and another location. One of these individuals was in the process

1. See Appendix A for sample letter.

of moving to a new home—as Arnett's research reports, young adults are highly mobile.[2] The Skype interviews averaged about the same amount of time per interview as face-to-face interviews and seemed to offer neither significant drawbacks nor advantages over in-person interviews.

OVERVIEW OF SAMPLE

This overview is intended to provide a landscape view of those who participated in the survey, drawing special attention to those who were interviewed. As is shown below, the group who was interviewed is representative of the larger group surveyed. This establishes validity for the responses they give in their interviews, not for the purposes of generalization, but in order to show that, as a group, they are in many ways representative of their demographic.

Age: Chronological and Psychological

There were two limiting factors in my study: chronological age and church involvement. All of those included in the final results are young adults who self-reported as being between the ages of eighteen and thirty when surveyed and interviewed. The following chart shows the frequency of distribution for the ages of those who took the survey. The average age for those who took the survey was 24.9 and the median age was 24. Unless otherwise noted, all of the following tables, charts, and graphs report data that was gathered on the 176 individuals who fit the sample frame for this research study.

2. Arnett, *Emerging Adulthood*, 11–12.

Chart C.1. What is your age today?

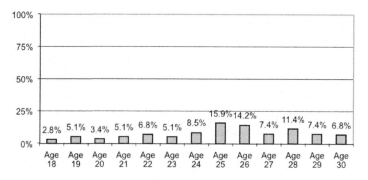

When analyzing the group of those interviewed, it turned out that there were no twenty-four or thirty year olds in the sample, and therefore the group interviewed actually consisted only of those between the ages of eighteen and twenty-nine.

Chart C.2. What is your age today? (30 Interviewees)

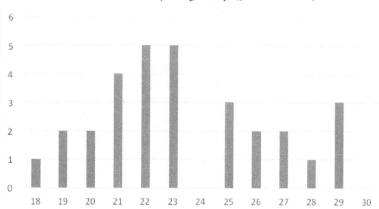

The average age for those interviewed was 23.4 and the median age was 23.5. We did not discuss their age during the interview; however, I was interested in their self-perceptions surrounding their age. In order to discover their psychological age I asked two questions through the survey.

Involvement in the PC(USA)

As mentioned above, survey respondents were filtered by their answers to two questions in addition to age. Those retained in the sample selected "PC(USA)" in answer to the question, "In what tradition were you raised?" or "How would you identify your religious identity today?" or both. All of those interviewed fit this sample as well. This means that some grew up in a PC(USA) church but no longer attend or have switched traditions. Some were raised in another tradition and got involved in a PC(USA) ministry or congregation during college or their young adult years. Some were raised in the PC(USA) and are still active members—singing in the choir or serving as an elder or deacon. They may or may not be official members "on the rolls," but they identify with the PC(USA). All are, or were at one time, "one of us."

I chose this range of levels of involvement and participation for the sample frame because I believe that these are the young adults from whom we can learn the most, and additionally, they are the ones to whom we are accountable.[3] Those who were a part of our body and have left can give us insight into the ways in which we are failing to reach out to young adults as well as the variety of places they are finding for spiritual growth. Those who have become involved recently or continue to be involved can give us insight into things the church is doing to nurture the faith of young adults. In response to sociological findings, it is also imperative to seek to understand the places where spiritual inquiry and growth as well as faith formation are happening for young adults who report high levels of interest in faith and low levels of "religiosity" according to standard scales.

It is also important to note that I chose to avoid interviewing any seminary students or pastors. I did, however, happen to interview one young woman who was interested in going to seminary in a few years and one young man who had attended seminary but dropped out after a year and a half. In addition to these two, one was married to a PC(USA) minister, one had a grandparent who was a minister, one had two parents who were ministers, and one had a parent who was a church organist. In total, four of those I interviewed have a familial relation who work, or at one time worked, in a PC(USA) congregation. At one point I considered avoiding doing interviews with anyone who had a parent or spouse who

---

3. In a theoretical sense the church is responsible to all people; however, for the purposes of this study, and in order to create a sample frame, I have chosen to limit interviews to those who are or were involved in the PC(USA).

was a PC(USA) minister. I chose not to use this filter because the reality is that many young adults are only one or two degrees separated from a minister in their own family, and by avoiding these individuals I would no longer have a representative sample of young adults who are connected with PC(USA) congregations.[4]

Gender

More women than men participated in the survey.[5] While the PC(USA) reflects a similar gender distribution, with more women as members of PC(USA) congregations than men,[6] I chose to pursue a balanced split for gender in this research. The rationale is that even if people are not attending church regularly, congregations are still interested in the way they practice and discuss their faith. Additionally, while the PC(USA) does not have a balanced gender split among members, elders, or ministers, this is the gender split for the population at large. To this end, I interviewed fifteen young men and fifteen young women.

Geographical Distribution: "Home," Current Residence, and Travel

The following map shows the geographical distribution of those who completed the survey. These results are compiled from the zip code they listed for their current residency, and the city and state they listed as where they were from. Due to a number of individuals who were moving between places when they took the survey, as well as a few who chose to skip the question, these results are incomplete. For example, one was walking the

4. Research Services, Presbyterian Church (USA), *Religious and Demographic Profile of Presbyterians, 2008.*

5. Fifty-one men (29 percent), 124 women (70.5 percent) and one transgendered individual took the survey. Because this research project is primarily focusing on the qualitative data collected through the interviews, little attention has been given to differences in gender. There were some differences between the genders—for example, women are slightly more interested in growing in faith—however, these findings will not be reported here.

6. Women are a majority of members (64 percent) and elders (52 percent), a quarter of pastors (27 percent), and 45 percent of specialized clergy in the PC(USA). Research Services, Presbyterian Church (USA), *Religious and Demographic Profile of Presbyterians, 2008*, 12.

Appalachian Trail and was unsure where he would be living when this hike was complete, and another had finished a summer internship at a national park in Alaska and was staying with his parents until he found more permanent housing.

Figure C.3. "What is your current address?"

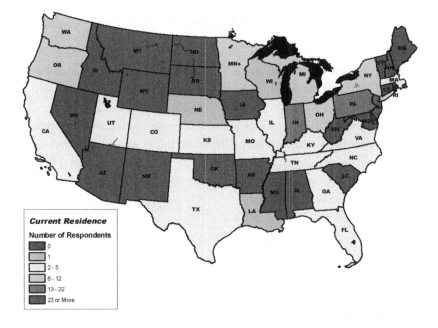

This map shows that the majority of those who participated in the survey currently live in the Northeast or Northwest.

The following map shows the distribution of the places these same young adults call "home." This map was compiled by the answers young adults provided to the question, "How do you answer the question, 'Where are you from?' when someone asks?" This map shows greater distribution across the South, Midwest, and Mountain West. This suggests that during their young adults years the movement of young adults condenses, perhaps (one may guess) from more rural to more urban settings.

Figure C.4. "Where do you call 'home'?"

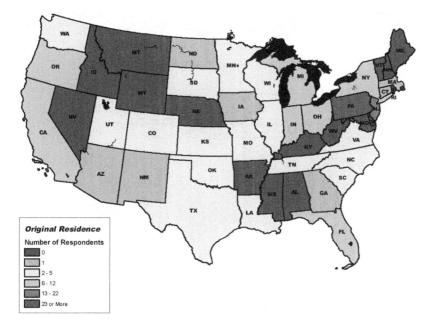

Those interviewed currently live in twelve different states and three countries other than the United States; one moved back to the United States the day before our interview. They called fifteen different states home. The individuals interviewed called one of the lower forty-eight states home and their current residences were concentrated in the Northeast and Midwest. The Northeast was the most densely represented in both interviews and surveys, which is likely explained by the reality that I currently lived in the Northeast during this project, and while I attempted to contact individuals from across the United States, I know more people in the Northeast, having lived here for eight of the past nine years.

Additionally, with regard to geography, I asked those participating in the survey to list the number of places they have lived in the last five years. The following table shows that the mean number of moves is 5.5, while the average is 3 (these were the same results for the group of individuals who were interviewed). The most anyone moved was eleven times and the least was none (totaling "one" residence). This confirms and gives greater detail to Arnett's finding regarding the high mobility of young adults contributing to the feeling of being "in between."[7] It also shows, however, that there are

7. Arnett, *Emerging Adulthood*, 11–12.

large numbers of individuals who are not highly mobile. About 14 percent of young adults (twenty-five in this survey) did not report moving at all in the last five years. Thirty percent had moved only twice.[8]

Table C.5. "List the places you have lived in the last five years."

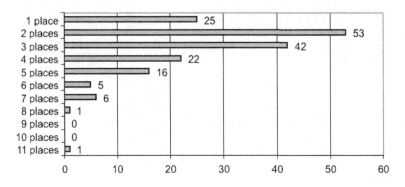

While Arnett is correct to point out that young adulthood is the most highly mobile time of life, this does not seem to be the case for every young adult. This may be explained in a number of ways. Young adults in higher numbers than previous generations are continuing to live at home with parents to save money. As we saw in chapter 1 as well, many are delaying marriage. The low numbers also may represent those in their earlier as opposed to later twenties, who have not yet had the opportunity to move.[9]

These young adults lived in all manner of places. Some were homeowners and lived with their spouse. Some lived in an apartment with roommates or a spouse. Some were living at home with parents while in transition from college to graduate school, or from work or study overseas to work in the States. Some had been living with their parents for the past few years while unemployed. Some lived in college or graduate school or military housing. Of those who were more mobile, many had spent a semester or longer in an international country. The list of places where they had lived included nearly all of the fifty states as well as thirty-one countries

---

8. This data has not been run through multiple regression analysis, which could potentially show a correlation between age and the number of times an individual has moved in the last five years.

9. Running a cross tabulation with respect to age and number of places lived would expose this data. For the purposes of this research study, however, it is sufficient to note that while young adults are generally "highly mobile," this is not the case for all young adults.

(including Kuwait, Iraq, Israel, Egypt, and Rwanda) on six continents.[10] Those interviewed represented nineteen states and eight countries. Their time in foreign countries was spent in military service, higher education, study abroad programs, volunteer mission work, and full-time employment. Between the time I initially contacted the young adults who were interviewed and the time we met about a quarter had moved—either permanently or between school and their parents' home.

Sexual Orientation and Marital Status

Four of the young men I interviewed were gay and one young woman marked her sexual orientation as "queer," stating that she had dated both men and women. Three shared this only through the online survey they participated in and two brought up their sexual orientation during our interview. I was somewhat surprised by these seemingly high numbers, as I did not seek out individuals with a homosexual orientation. This may be explained in a number of ways. First, the PC(USA) may be one of the religious havens for those who are homosexual; indeed, the denomination's policy changes show their openness and affirmation of this population. Second, my sample may have unintentionally happened upon a larger number of LGBTQ individuals. Third, the statistics for the LGBTQ community are higher than the public assumes, and my sample is actually somewhat random and representative of the population at large. I believe any of these could provide a reasonable explanation. The following table shows the frequency distribution of the sexual orientation for the 176 individuals in the survey. The "Frequency" column reports the actual numbers of people who made a selection.

---

10. In no particular order the countries where these young adults reported living over the last five years includes Kuwait, Iraq, New Zealand, Rwanda, Great Britain, Canada, various countries in the Mediterranean, Israel, Mexico, India, Northern Ireland, Ethiopia, Scotland, Italy, Ecuador, Spain, South Korea, China, Singapore, the Dominican Republic, Australia, France, Lebanon, Egypt, Kenya, South Africa, Turkey, and Tanzania.

Table C.6. "How would you describe your sexual orientation?"

		Frequency	Percent
Valid	Straight	166	94.3
	Gay	4	2.3
	Bisex-ual	3	1.7
	Queer	2	1.1
	Total	175	99.4
Miss-ing	System	1	.6
	Total	176	100.0

If LGBTQ individuals made up 13 percent of those I interviewed, it appears as though I have a slight oversampling compared with the online survey, of which only about 6 percent are not straight. Both of these, however, fall within the range of estimates given for the number of individuals who are in the LGBT (Lesbian Gay Bisexual and Transgender) community within the United States.[11]

Four of those interviewed were married—two men and two women. One had been married less than a year and the others had been married more than two years. Of these, as well as the rest of those interviewed, none reported having children.

Race

Two of the young women I interviewed identified as African American, one of whom added that she was half-black and half-Cherokee. One young man identified half-Latino and half-Caucasian, and the majority of those interviewed (twenty-seven) were Caucasian. I did not go out of my way to seek a balance in race for this study; however, those interviewed did reflect the demographic landscape of the PC(USA) with the exception of

11. The 2000 census found that less than 1 percent of American households is homosexual; however, Gallup found that Americans believe that 1 in every 5 individuals is gay. This large spectrum suggests that it is impossible to make any claims about the gay population being over- or underrepresented in this research. Most of the data on this topic is based on perceptions and speculation. Robinson, "What Percentage of the Population Is Gay?"; Leff, "Gay Population in U.S. Estimated at 4 Million, Gary Gates Says."

any Asian representation.[12] Those interviewed reflect the numbers of those who participated in the survey as is shown in the chart below.

Chart C.7. "How would you describe your racial or ethnic background?"

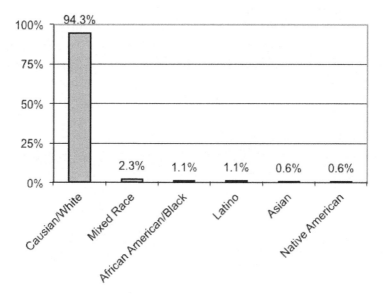

Education, Vocation, and Income

I additionally asked about the highest level of education they had completed, sources and amount of income, and current employment status. Of the thirty interviewed two reported that the highest level of education they had completed was a high school diploma, ten reported attending some college (most were partway through a four-year degree, although a few had not yet completed their two- or four-year degree program), eleven had completed a college-level degree, and eight were enrolled in or had completed postgraduate work.

Of those interviewed two were unemployed, three work in retail sales, three were teachers, two performed in the fine arts (an actor and

12 Most Presbyterians are white (members, 96 percent; elders, 95 percent; pastors, 92 percent; specialized clergy, 89 percent) with minimal distribution throughout other ethnic groups. Research Services, Presbyterian Church (USA), *Religious and Demographic Profile of Presbyterians*, iv.

a dancer), two worked in communications, one worked in health care, one was an attorney and city council member, one worked for the federal government, and fifteen reported being students. Of those interviewed two were connected with the military—one about to join and the other a spouse of an enlisted man.

In response to the question, "What is your approximate income from all sources of funding (income, loans, parents, etc.)?" thirteen selected $1–25,000, nine selected $25,000–50,000, one selected $50,000-$100,000, three selected $100,000–200,000 and one selected more than $200,000 (for the individual selecting this category the income came from a trust). Two chose to abstain from answering this question.

Regarding the sources of income nine reported at least 97 percent of their income coming from personal income. The second largest source of income was from parents, then student loans. Fifteen (half of those interviewed) reported receiving some portion of income from their parents. For the five receiving student loans, this made up between 50 and 100 percent of their income.

BIBLIOGRAPHY

Arias, Elizabeth, Jiaquan Xu, and Kenneth D. Kochanek. "United States Life Tables, 2016." National Vital Statistics Report, May 7, 2019. https://www.cdc.gov/nchs/data/nvsr/nvsr68/nvsr68_04-508.pdf.

Aquinas, Thomas, Saint. *Summa Theologia I-II*, 94.

Arnett, Jeffrey Jensen. *Emerging Adulthood: The Winding Road from the Late Teens through the Twenties*. New York: Oxford, 2004.

Augustine, Saint. *On Christian Teaching*. Translated by R. P. H. Green. New York: Oxford University Press, 2008.

Barth, Karl. *Church Dogmatics*. II.1: *The Doctrine of God*. Edited by G. W. Bromiley and T. F. Torrance. Edinburgh: T&T Clark, 2000.

———. *Church Dogmatics*. III.2: *The Doctrine of Creation*. Edited by G. W. Bromiley and T. F. Torrance. Edinburgh: T&T Clark, 2010.

———. *Church Dogmatics*. IV.3.2: *The Doctrine of Reconciliation*. Edited by G. W. Bromiley and T. F. Torrance. Edinburgh: T&T Clark, 1962.

Bass, Dorothy C., ed. *Practicing Our Faith: A Way of Life for a Searching People*. 2nd ed. San Francisco: Jossey-Bass, 2010.

———. *Receiving the Day: Christian Practices for Opening the Gift of Time*. San Francisco: Jossey-Bass, 2001.

Belenky, Mary Field, et al. *Women's Ways of Knowing: The Development of Self, Voice, and Mind*. 10th anniversary ed. New York: Basic Books, 1997.

Berryman, Jerome. *Godly Play: A Way of Religious Education*. San Francisco: Harper, 1991.

Bourdieu, Pierre. *Distinction: A Social Critique of the Judgement of Taste*. Cambridge: Harvard University Press, 1987.

Brooks, David, "The Odyssey Years." *New York Times*, October 9, 2007. https://www.nytimes.com/2007/10/09/opinion/09brooks.html.

Brown, Frank Burch. *Good Taste, Bad Taste, and Christian Taste: Aesthetics in Religious Life*. New York: Oxford, 2003.

Brown, Stuart, and Christopher Vaughan. *Play: How It Shapes the Brain, Opens the Imagination, and Invigorates the Soul*. New York: Avery, 2010.

Bushnell, Horace. *Christian Nurture*. 1860. Reprint, Whitefish, MT: Kessinger, 2010.

Calvin, John. *Institutes of the Christian Religion*. 2 vols. Philadelphia: Westminster, 1960.

Chaves, Mark. *Congregations in America*. Cambridge: Harvard University Press, 2004.

Creswell, John W. *Qualitative Inquiry and Research Design: Choosing among Five Traditions*. Thousand Oaks, CA: Sage, 1997.

Dankosky, John. "Emerging Adults." *Where We Live*, February 28, 2011. https://www.wnpr.org/post/emerging-adults.

Davies, Robertson. *What's Bred in the Bone*. New York: Penguin, 1986.

De Gruchy, John W. *Christianity, Art and Transformation: Theological Aesthetics in the Struggle for Justice*. 1st ed. Cambridge: Cambridge University Press, 2008.

Dewey, John. *Art as Experience*. New York: Perigee, 2005.

———. *Democracy and Education*. New York: Macmillan, 1944.

———. *The Later Works, 1925–1953*. Vol. 12, *1938, Logic: The Theory of Inquiry*, edited by Jo Ann Boydston. Carbondale: Southern Illinois University Press, 2008.

Dillenberger, John. *A Theology of Artistic Sensibilities: The Visual Arts and the Church*. 1986. Reprint, Eugene, OR: Wipf & Stock, 2004.

Douglass, Katherine M. "Aesthetic Learning Theory and the Faith Formation of Young Adults." *Religious Education* 108 (2013) 449–66.

———. Review of *Choosing Our Religion*, by Elizabeth Drescher. *Theology Today* 74 (2017) 193–94.

Drescher, Elizabeth. *Choosing Our Religion: The Spiritual Lives of America's Nones*. New York: Oxford University Press, 2016.

Drury, Amanda. "'I Have Seen and I Testify': An Articulacy Theory of Testimony in Adolescent Spiritual Development." PhD diss., Princeton Theological Seminary, 2012.

Dykstra, Craig. *Growing in the Life of Faith: Education and Christian Practices*. 2nd ed. Louisville: Westminster John Knox, 2005.

Elder, Glen H., Jr. *Children of the Great Depression: Social Change in Life Experience*. 25th anniversary ed. Boulder, CO: Westview, 1998.

———. "The Life Course as Developmental Theory." *Child Development* 69 (1998) 1–12.

Erikson, Erik H. *Identity and the Life Cycle*. New York: Norton, 1994.

Flory, Richard, and Donald E. Miller. *Finding Faith: The Spiritual Quest of the Post-Boomer Generation*. New Brunswick: Rutgers University Press, 2008.

Fowler, James. *Stages of Faith: The Psychology of Human Development and the Quest for Meaning*. San Francisco: Harper & Row, 1981.

Furstenberg, Frank F. "Family Change in Global Perspective: How and Why Family Systems Change." University of Pennsylvania Population Center Working Paper (PSC/PARC), March 25, 2019. https://repository.upenn.edu/psc_publications/22/.

Gadamer, Hans-Georg. *Truth and Method*. 2nd rev. ed. London: Continuum, 2006.

Gardner, Howard. *Frames of Mind: The Theory of Multiple Intelligences*. New York: Basic Books, 1983.

Gill, Theodore A. "Barth and Mozart." *Theology Today* 43 (1986) 403–11.

Goto, Courtney Teru. "Artistic Play: Seeking the God of the Unexpected." PhD diss., Emory University, 2010.

Greene, Maxine. *The Dialectic of Freedom*. John Dewey Lecture. New York: Teachers College Press, 1988.

———. *Releasing the Imagination: Essays on Education, the Arts, and Social Change*. San Francisco: Jossey-Bass, 2000.

———. *Variations on a Blue Guitar: The Lincoln Center Institute Lectures on Aesthetic Education*. New York: Teachers College Press, 2001.

Gunter, Mary Alice, Thomas H. Estes, and Susan L. Mintz. *Instruction: A Models Approach.* Boston: Allyn & Bacon, 2006.

hooks, bell. *Teaching to Transgress: Education as the Practice of Freedom.* New York: Routledge, 1994.

Hutchison, Elizabeth D. *Dimensions of Human Behavior: The Changing Life Course.* 4th ed. Thousand Oaks, CA: Sage, 2010.

Jenkins, Henry. *Confronting the Challenges of Participatory Culture: Media Education for the 21st Century.* Cambridge: MIT Press, 2009.

Jones, Gavin W., and Wei-Jun Jean Yeung. "Marriage in Asia." *Journal of Family Issues* 35 (2014) 1567–83.

Jones, Jeffrey M. "US Church Membership Down Sharply in Past Two Decades." Gallup, April 18, 2019. https://news.gallup.com/poll/248837/church-membership-down-sharply-past-two-decades.aspx.

Kant, Immanuel. *Critique of the Power of Judgment.* Edited by Paul Guyer. Translated by Paul Guyer and Eric Matthews. New York: Cambridge University Press, 2001.

Lane, Rose Wilder. *Woman's Day Book of American Needlework.* New York: Simon & Schuster, 1963.

Leff, Lisa. "Gay Population in U.S. Estimated at 4 Million, Gary Gates Says." *Huffington Post,* April 7, 2011. http://www.huffingtonpost.com/2011/04/07/gay-population-us-estimate_n_846348.html.

Levine, Faythe, and Cortney Heimerl. *Handmade Nation: The Rise of DIY, Art, Craft, and Design.* New York: Princeton Architectural Press, 2008.

Lewis, William F. *Marketing Research: A Decision-Making Approach.* 10th ed. Dayton, OH: UD Printing & Design, 2011.

Loder, James E. *The Logic of the Spirit: Human Development in Theological Perspective.* San Francisco: Jossey-Bass, 1998.

McCracken, Brett. *Hipster Christianity: When Church and Cool Collide.* Grand Rapids: Baker, 2010.

Merritt, Carol Howard. *Tribal Church: Ministering to the Missing Generation.* Herndon, VA: Alban Institute, 2007.

Mezirow, Jack. *Transformative Dimensions of Adult Learning.* San Francisco: Jossey-Bass, 1991.

Milliner, Matthew. "A Vacation for Grünewald: On Karl Barth's Vexed Relationship with Visual Art." *Princeton Theological Review* 8 (2007) 5–16.

Moltmann, Jurgen. *The Trinity and the Kingdom.* Minneapolis: Fortress, 1993.

National Public Radio. "Losing Our Religion: The Growth of the 'Nones.'" *Morning Edition,* January 13, 2013. http://www.npr.org/blogs/thetwo-way/2013/01/14/169164840/losing-our-religion-the-growth-of-the-nones.

Newman, Katherine S. *The Accordion Family: Boomerang Kids, Anxious Parents, and the Private Toll of Global Competition.* Boston: Beacon, 2012.

———. "Ties That Bind: Cultural Interpretations of Delayed Adulthood in Western Europe and Japan." *Sociological Forum* 23 (2008) 645–69.

Newport, Frank "Why Are Americans Losing Respect for Organized Religion?" Gallup News, July 16, 2019. https://news.gallup.com/opinion/polling-matters/260738/why-americans-losing-confidence-organized-religion.aspx.

Osborne, William. "Marketplace of Ideas: But First, the Bill; A Personal Commentary on American and European Cultural Funding." Originally published by *ArtsJournal.com,* March 11, 2004. http://www.osborne-conant.org/arts_funding.htm.

Osmer, Richard R. *Practical Theology: An Introduction*. Grand Rapids: Eerdmans, 2008.

Pannenberg, Wolfhart. *Systematic Theology*. Vol. 2. Translated by Geoffrey W. Bromiley. Grand Rapids: Eerdmans, 1994.

Pew Forum on Religion and Public Life. *"Nones" on the Rise: One-in-Five Adults Have No Religious Affiliation*. Washington, DC: Pew Research Center, 2012.

———. *Religion among Millenials: Less Religiously Active than Older Americans, but Fairly Traditional in Other Ways*. Washington, DC: Pew Research Center, 2010.

Pew Research Center. *Millenials: A Portrait of Generation Next; Confident. Connected. Open to Change*. Edited by Paul Taylor and Scott Keeter. February 2010. https://www.pewresearch.org/wp-content/uploads/sites/3/2010/10/millennials-confident-connected-open-to-change.pdf.

———. *Recession Turns a Graying Office Grayer*. September 3, 2009. https://www.pewsocialtrends.org/2009/09/03/recession-turns-a-graying-office-grayer/.

Piaget, Jean. *Play, Dreams and Imitation in Childhood*. New York: Norton, 1962.

Putnam, Robert D. *Bowling Alone: The Collapse and Revival of American Community*. New York: Simon & Schuster, 2001.

Putnam, Robert D., and David E. Campbell. *American Grace: How Religion Divides and Unites Us*. New York: Simon & Schuster, 2010.

Rabin, Roni Caryn. "Put a Ring on It? Millennial Couples Are in No Hurry." *New York Times*, May 29, 2018. https://www.nytimes.com/2018/05/29/well/mind/millennials-love-marriage-sex-relationships-dating.html.

Research Services, Presbyterian Church (USA). *Religious and Demographic Profile of Presbyterians, 2008: Findings from the Initial Survey of the 2009–2011 Presbyterian Panel*. Louisville: Presbyterian Church (USA), 2009.

Ricoeur, Paul. *Interpretation Theory: Discourse and the Surplus of Meaning*. Fort Worth: Texas Christian University Press, 1976.

Roberts, Alexander, James Donaldson, and A. Cleveland Coxe, eds. *Ante-Nicene Fathers*. Vol. 1, *Apostolic Fathers, Justin Martyr, Irenaeus*. Grand Rapids: Eerdmans, 1950.

Robison, Jennifer. "What Percentage of the Population Is Gay?" Gallup News, October 8, 2002. http://www.gallup.com/poll/6961/what-percentage-population-gay.aspx.

Root, Andrew. *Revisiting Relational Youth Ministry: From a Strategy of Influence to a Theology of Incarnation*. Downers Grove: IVP, 2007.

Rorty, Richard. "Overcoming the Tradition: Heidegger and Dewey." *The Review of Metaphysics* 30 (1976) 280–305.

Rush, David. "Talking Back: A Model for Postperformance Discussion of New Plays." *Theatre Topics* 10 (2000) 53–63.

Sayers, Dorothy L. *The Mind of the Maker*. New York: Continuum, 2005.

Scherger, Simone. "Social Change and the Timing of Family Transitions in West Germany: Evidence from Cohort Comparisons." *Time & Society* 18 (2009) 106–29.

Sigler, Shannon. "Lap Full of Words." Seattle, Washington, 2017.

Sloan, Wilona M. "Making Content Connections through Arts Integration." *ASCD Education Update* 51 (2009). http://www.ascd.org/publications/newsletters/education-update/mar09/vol51/num03/Making-Content-Connections-Through-Arts-Integration.aspx.

Smith, Christian, and Melinda Lundquist Denton. *Soul Searching: The Religious and Spiritual Lives of American Teenagers*. New York: Oxford University Press, 2009.

Smith, Christian, and Patricia Snell. *Souls in Transition: The Religious and Spiritual Lives of Emerging Adults*. New York: Oxford University Press, 2005.

Smith, David I., and James K. A. Smith, eds. *Teaching and Christian Practices: Reshaping Faith and Learning.* Grand Rapids: Eerdmans, 2011.

Swanson, Elizabeth. *Eden.* Theater Intime, Princeton University, Princeton, New Jersey, December 13, 2011.

Tanner, Kathryn. *Christ the Key.* Cambridge: Cambridge University Press, 2010.

Twenge, Jean, *iGen: Why Today's Super-Connected Kids Are Growing Up Less Rebellious, More Tolerant, Less Happy—and Completely Unprepared for Adulthood.* New York: Atria Paperback, 2017.

U.S. Census Bureau. "Estimated Median Age at First Marriage, by Sex: 1890 to Present." https://www.census.gov/data/tables/time-series/demo/families/marital.html.

Van Huyssteen, Wentzel. *Alone in the World? Human Uniqueness in Science and Technology.* Grand Rapids: Eerdmans, 2006.

Vygotsky, L. S. *Mind in Society: The Development of Higher Psychological Processes.* Edited by Michael Cole et al. Cambridge: Harvard University Press, 1978.

Westerhoff, John H. *Will Our Children Have Faith?* Rev. ed. Harrisburg, PA: Morehouse, 2000.

Wuthnow, Robert J. *After the Baby Boomers: How Twenty- and Thirty-Somethings Are Shaping the Future of American Religion.* Princeton: Princeton University Press, 2010.

———. *All in Sync: How Music and Art Are Revitalizing American Religion.* Berkeley: University of California Press, 2006.

———. *Arts and Religion Survey 1999 [United States].* Version Date: January 28, 2016. https://www.icpsr.umich.edu/icpsrweb/NADAC/studies/35192.

———. "Taking Talk Seriously: Religious Discourse as Social Practice." *Journal for the Scientific Study of Religion* 50 (2011) 1–21.

Yen, Hope. "Census: Recession Taking Toll on Young Adults." Associated Press, September 22, 2011.

Zirsky, Andrew. *Beyond the Screen: Youth Ministry for the Connected but Alone Generation.* Nashville: Abingdon, 2015.

Made in the USA
Coppell, TX
16 April 2022

76666865R10090